CEYLON
AND THE HOLLANDERS
1658-1796

THE NAVARATNA MEDAL, 1686.

CEYLON
AND THE HOLLANDERS
1658-1796

BY

P. E. PIERIS

DERANIYAGALA SAMARASINHA SRIWARDHANA

D. Litt. (Cantab.) Ceylon Civil Service. Vice-President,
Royal Asiatic Society (Ceylon.)

GYAN

Published by

Gyan Publishing House
5, Ansari Road
Daryaganj, New Delhi-110002
Phone: 011-47034999, 9811692060
E-mail: books@gyanbooks.com

Distribution Network
gyanbooks.com
India, USA, Canada, UK, Australia, France

ISBN : 978-81-212-3211-1 (PB)
First Published, 1918

2nd Impression 2020

Printed at: Gyan Press, Delhi.

Ceylon and The Hollanders
1658-1796
Author: P. E. Pieris

CEYLON AND THE HOLLANDERS

1658 - 1796

BY

P. E. PIERIS

DERANIYAGALA SAMARASINHA SRIWARDHANA

D. Litt. (Cantab.) Ceylon Civil Service. Vice-President, Royal Asiatic Society (Ceylon.)

AMERICAN CEYLON MISSION PRESS.
TELLIPPALAI, CEYLON.
1918.

TO

THE HON. SIR ANTON BERTRAM, Kt. K. C.

Chief Justice of Ceylon,

who, East of Suez, finely upholds

the Cambridge Tradition,

this book

is Respectfully Dedicated.

"Where there is no vision, the people perish."

INTRODUCTION

Many visitors from Europe since Saar of Nuremberg (1647-1658) have left on record their experiences in Ceylon during the time of the Netherlands East India Company, and the most important of these narratives have been translated into English and published from time to time. Much information is contained in the pages of various Journals and Magazines, and an important series of seven Memoirs, issued since 1903 by the learned Government Archivist and his able Assistant, Mrs. Anthonisz, has shed a great deal of light on the administration and policy of the Company till 1740. Sir Alexander Johnston, Chief Justice of Ceylon from 1811 to 1819, left behind a valuable collection of manuscripts, much of which has been rendered accessible to me through the great kindness of Mr. A. W. Winter of Baddegama. In addition, private documents in Sinhalese Walauwas throw an interesting and personal sidelight on the period. Out of this material the present compilation has been made, in the hope that it will furnish the average inhabitant of Ceylon who can read English with a co-herent, reasonably accurate, and perhaps not uninteresting account of his country during its transition from the mediaeval to the modern. The

Medal shown in the Frontispiece was very kindly placed at my disposal by Mr. H. de O. Ekanayaka of Matara.

This book is the sequel to another, Ceylon and the Portuguese, written for publication in England. Though the issue of this latter has been delayed by war conditions, the reader has been treated as not unfamiliar with its contents.

THE JUDGE'S HOUSE,
JAFFNA.

P. E. P.

CONTENTS

CHAPTER I

A conspiracy against the Company. Its territory. Principles of administration. Condition of the country. Agriculture. New industries. Justice. Conversion. The Lascarins. The Burghers. Inter-marriage. Anxiety for peace. Attitude of Raja Sinha. The British. A conspiracy against the King. Its failure. Van Goens as Governor. The Company prosperous. The French Company. The Nayaker of Madura.

CHAPTER II

Arandora captured. Embassy of Bystervelt. The French at Trincomalee. Count de Lanerolle. Bibilegama captured. Clement Magellian. Tennekon Disava. Ambanwela Rala. The King's pleasantries. Treachery of Tennekon. The Wanni. Laurens Pyl as Governor. The Company's policy. Raja Sinha and his subjects. Hanguranketa. The King's diversions. His religious attitude. His partiality for Europeans. Attempts to keep him in humour. Obsequiousness of Pyl. Hendrik van Rheede. The King's abdication. The memorial celebration.

CHAPTER III

Wimala Daham Surya. The city of Colombo. Navaratna. Policy of the new King. Attitude of the Company. Buddhism. The clergy. Thomas van Rhee. The Chaliyas. The Elephant hunt. Arecanuts. Jaffna. Changarapillai. Character of the Tamils. Encroachment on tanks. Unrest in Jaffna. The Ports opened. The Buddhist Ordination. Friendly attitude of the Court. Administration of the Kingdom. Military measures. Subserviency of the Company. Administration of Justice. Cornelis Joan Simons. The Thesawalamai. Death of Wimala Daham Surya.

CHAPTER IV

Narendra Sinha. The Ports closed. Governor Becker's reforms. Condition of the Public Service. Wijayawardhana Mudaliyar. Salt and cinnamon. Jaffna. Conspiracy against the King. Misconduct of de Bevere. The King friendly. Augustin Rumpf. Trade disputes. Smuggling. The Chalias. Misgovernment of Vuyst. Versluys. Pielat as Commissioner. Narendra Sinha's administration. Unrest. Reform of abuses. The Law Courts. Van Domburg. Rioting among the Chalias. General discontent. The Council helpless. Lewke Disava. Arrival of Van Imhoff.

CHAPTER V

Sri Wijaya Raja Sinha. Van Imhoff's policy. Agriculture. Buddhism. Saranankara. Sinhalese literature. The religious revival. Roman Catholic missionaries. Mission to Pegu. Trade disputes. Smuggling. Rioting. Mission to Siam. Accession of Kirti Sri Raja Sinha. The British. The King's religious policy. The Ordination restored. Lienderan de Saram. Government of Loten. Jan Schreuder.

CHAPTER VI

Review of the Company's administration. Classes of its subjects. Nepotism. Dishonesty. Legal administration. The Land Raad. The Portuguese Tombo. The New Tombo. Classes of lands. The native officials. Bribery over their appointments. Their remuneration. Misuse of the Company's lands. Badawedili lands. The Company's dues. The Pearl Fishery. Other sea revenue. Wijayawardhana. Coffee. Cardamoms. Pepper. Arecanut. Smuggling. Coconut and arrack. The Leper Asylum. Conversion. Persecution of the heathen. Indifference of the clergy. The Seminaries. The Catholic missionaries. The resistance of the Catholics. Criticism of the clergy. Immorality of the Europeans. The Scholarchal Commission. Education under the Company.

CHAPTER VII

The King's marriages. The Malabar influence. Dumbara Rala and the Company. Greed for cinnamon. Consequent obsequiousness of the Company. Desertions. Trade jealousy. Growth of a stronger policy at Court. Policy regarding cinnamon. Secret policy against the King. Attitude of the Company's subjects. Unrest among them. Rioting. A conspiracy against the King. He supports the rioters. Open war. Matara and Hanwella captured. Guerrilla tactics of the Sinhalese. Company anxious for peace. Letter to the King. Arrival of Baron van Eck as Governor. Pybus' Mission. Description of the Capital. The reception of an ambassador. Method of conversation. Failure of the Mission.

CHAPTER VIII

Chilaw and Puttalam occupied. Failure of a fresh expedition. Further preparations. Illangakon Maha Mudaliyar. The new campaign. The Capital occupied. The attack on Hanguranketa. Withdrawal of van Eck. His death. The garrison blockaded. Moyaart summoned from Jaffna. Arrival of Falck as Governor. Energetic steps taken by him. The Treaty of Colombo. Falck's intrigues. The Treaty ratified. Cost of the war. Trouble with the Thever. Chilaw. Puttalam. The salt industry. Batticaloa. Jaffna. The Mutu Raja Wela scheme. Canals. Hena cultivation. Planting cinnamon.

CHAPTER IX

The Disawa and his duties. Policy towards the Mudaliyars. Attitude towards Sinhalese prejudices. Pseudo Burghers. Caste duties. Sumptuary regulations. Buddhism tolerated. Roman Catholics. Wolfs of Mecklenburg. The Tamils. Purchase of titles. Domestic habits. Embassy to Batavia, The Tooth Relic restored. The Buddhist revival. Anxiety of the Company. Literature at Court. Literature in the South. Jeux d' esprit. Metrical Diagrams. The King and the Company. The supply of salt. The Wanni. The British at Trincomalee. Hugh Boyd. Death of the King. Military preparations. Death of Falck. Abayasinha Maha Mudaliyar. Treaty with the Nawab. The British and the United Provinces. Unrest. De Meuron in Sabaragamuwa.

CHAPTER X

Attitude of the Company. Development of cinnamon planting. Medals. Weakness of Sinhalese for Medals. Agriculture and Irrigation. The Giant's Tank. The Negumbo canal. The areca trade. The elephant hunt. Cotton cultivation. The Public Service. The condition of the Sinhalese. Social changes. Jaffna. The Sinhalese Kingdom. The Exchange Problem. Outbreak of hostilities in Europe. Departure of van der Graaf. The British and the piece goods trade. Holland invaded. British capture Trincomalee. Robert Andrews at Court. Jaffna occupied. Dumbara Rala at Madras. Preparations at Colombo. The de Meuron Regiment. Colombo threatened. Condition of the Hollanders. The enemy before Colombo. Negociations. End of the Company's rule.

AUTHORITIES RELIED ON.

Ceylon, Account of, by

Johann Jacob Saar of Nuremberg, (1647-1658), tr. by Ph. Freudenberg, R. A. S. Ceylon xi.

Philip Baldaeus, (1656-1665) Amsterdam 1672, tr. in Churchill's Voyages, iii.

Robert Knox, (1659-1679) London 1681.

Wouter Schouten of Haarlem, (1661-1664) tr. by Ph. Freudenberg. R. A. S. Cey. xi.

Albrecht Herport of Berne, (1663-1665) tr. by ? I. Cey. Lit. Reg.

Christoph Schweitzer of Wurtemberg, (1675-1682) tr. by S. L. London 1700.

Aegidius Daalmans of Antwerp, (1687-1689) tr. by D. W Ferguson. R. A. S. Cey. x.

Christoph Langhansz of Breslau, (1695-1696) tr. by D. W. Ferguson, iii Cey. Lit. Reg.

Johan Christopel Wolfs of Mecklenburg, (1749-1768) tr. by ? London 1785.

Charles Peter Thunberg of Upsala, (1777-1778) in Travels in Europe, Africa and Asia. London 1796.

Paul Eschelskroon, (1782 ?) appended to the English tr. of Wolfs.

Jacob Haafner of Halle (1782-1784) tr. fom a French tr. by D. W. Ferguson, v Cey. Lit. Reg.
Travels on Foot through Ceylon, tr. by ? London 1821.

Robert Percival, 1796 London.

Anthony Bertolacci, London 1817.

John Davy (1816-1820) London 1821.

From Welsh's Military Reminiscences, reprinted ii Cey. Lit. Reg.

H. Suckling ("An Officer, late of the Ceylon Rifles") London 1876.

Memorie of

Ryclof Van Goens, Jr., (1675-1679), tr. by Sophia Pieters, Colombo, 1910.

Thomas Van Rhee, (1692-1697), tr. by S. Pieters, Colombo, 1915.

Hendrick Zwardecroon, (1694-1697), do do, 1911

Cornelis Joan Simons, (1703-1907), do (Sophia Anthonisz) Colombo, 1914

Hendrick Becker, (1707-1716), do do, 1914

Jacob Christian Pielat, (1732-1734), do do 1905

Gustaaf Willem Baron Van Imhoff, (1736-1740), do do 1911

Julius Valentyn Stein Van Gollenesse, (1743-1751), Johnston *Mss.* tr. by?

Jan Schreuder, (1757-1762), Johnston *Mss.* tr. by?

Willem Jacob Van de Graaf, (1778-1794), Tr. by ? 1 Cey. Lit. Reg.

Burnand, once Chief of Batticaloa, 1809, iii,iv. Monthly Lit. Reg.

Diary of

Bystervelt's Embassy, 1671, tr. by F. H. de Vos, Jr., R. A. S. Cey. XI.

Gerrit de Heere, 1697, tr. by Sophia Anthonisz, Colombo 1914.

Schnee's Embassy, 1731, by Wijayasriwardhana Maha Mudiyanse, tr. by P. E. Pieris, R. A. S. Cey. XXI.

Kirti Sri Raja Sinha's Embassy to Siam, 1751, tr. by P. E. Pieris, R. A. S. Cey. XVIII.

Pybus' Embassy, 1762.

Van Eck's Expedition, 1765, tr. by A. E. Buultjens, R. A. S. Cey. XVI.

Iman Willem Falck, 1767, (report on circuit) Johnston *Mss.*

Boyd's Embassy, 1782, printed in the Miscellaneous Works of Hugh Boyd, edited by Lawrence Campbell, 2 vols, London, 1800.

Don Adrian de Alwis, Mudaliyar, 1774-1794, in Some Sinhalese Families, by P. E. Pieris.

Andrew's Embassy, (1795-1796), Ed. by J. P. Lewis, C M. G. R. A. S. Cey. XXVI.

Dagh Register, Batavia, 1661, Extracts from, tr. by F. H. de Vos, IV. Cey. Lit. Reg.

Report on

The Chalias, by Johannes Stafforts to Governor de Heere, c. 1700, Johnston *Mss.*

The Colombo Disawani, by G. L. de Coste, Disawa, 1770, Johnston *Mss.*

Puttalam District, by Elias Paravacini di Capelli, 1775, Johnston *Mss.*

Chilaw District, by Drieberg, 1798? Johnston *Mss.*

The Peace Negociations, by Governor Falck, March 1766, Johnston *Mss.*

Kantalai Tank, by J. G. Fornbauer, 1793, tr. by George Lee, i Cey. Lit. Reg.

The Pearl Fishery, by George Lee, (1658-1797) ii,iii. Cey. Lit. Reg.

The Dutch Records, by R. G. Anthonisz, Colombo 1907.

The Education Establishments of the Dutch, by J. D. Palm, R. A. S. Cey. 1846-7.

The Dutch Church in Ceylon, by J. D. Palm, R. A. S. Cey. 1847-8.

Correspondence,

Regarding Muturajawela, iii Cey. Lit. Reg.

The Surrender of Colombo, iii Cey. Lit. Reg.

With the Br. East India Company, (1788-1795) iv Cey. Lit. Reg.

Of Raja Sinha ii, tr. by D. W. Ferguson, R. A. S. Cey. xviii.

J. G. Van Angelbeek to the Governor at Fort William, June 1797, Johnston *Mss.*

Manuscripts

Illangakon, Sinhalese and Dutch, various.

Tilakaratna, Dutch, various.

In European Languages in the India Office, by C. C. Blagden, London 1916.

Sinhalese, in the British Museum, by D. M. de Zilva Wickremesinghe, London, 1900.

Extracts from the Wellesley, by A. E. Buultjens, iii Cey. Lit. Reg.

Resolutions of Council, various, Johnston *Mss.*

Rajawaliya, continued up to 1815, palm leaf, with Mr. L. A. Samarakkoddy, Advocate.

Goens, ... Instructions by Rycklof van, (1653—1661), tr. by Sophia Pieters, Colombo, 1908

Joinville, ... Narrative of the Negociations of the Court of Kandy with the British Government of Ceylon, by Joseph, tr. by W. Tolfrey, Johnston *Mss.*

Tombe, ... The surrender of Colombo, by C. F. de La, tr. by N. (Mrs. C. A. Lorensz) v Cey. Lit. Reg.

Strachan ... Elephants in Zeylan, by, extracted from Philosophical Transactions xxiii, 1704, Printed in ii Cey. Lit. Reg.

Alwis, ... Introduction to the Sidath Sangarawa, by James de, Colombo, 1852.

Petch, ... Grimm's Laboratorium Ceylonium, by T., in Ceylon Antiquary, vol. iii.

Ferguson, ... Joan Gideon Loten, by D. W., R. A. S. Cey. xix.

Tibbatuwawe ... The Mahawansa, continuation of, by, Maha Nayaka Unanse, c. 1775 tr. by L. C. Wijesinghe, Colombo.

Beknopte Historie, (1602-1757), anonymous, Colombo 1760, tr. by ? R. A. S. Cey. xi

O Oriente Portugues, Goa.

Upham ... Sacred and Historical Books of Ceylon, edited by Edward, 3 vols. London 1833.

Lawrie ... Gazeteer of the Central Province, by Sir A. C., 2 vols., Colombo, 1896.

GLOSSARY

Adigar, originally a judicial officer, but later applied to the two chief Ministers of the King.

Adukku, cooked provisions supplied to an official.

Aldear, from Port *Aldea,* a village.

Andi, the Indian fakir.

Amu, the *Varaku* of the Tamil, an inferior grain.

Amunam, as a dry measure, equals between 4½ and 6 bushels. The extent required to sow an amunam of seed was the chief unit of superficial measurement; while usually 24000 nuts formed an amunam of areca.

Appuhami, highborn men of the position of the sons of Mudaliyars.

Attapattu, originally the selected troops who formed the King's Guard.

Badawedili, Dutch *Accommodessan,* lands given to public servants for their maintenance while in office.

Bana, the doctrine of the Buddha.

Basnayaka, a high native official, acting as the mouthpiece of the European official.

Bo, the *ficus religiosa,* under which the Buddha attained perfect knowledge.

Bulat Surulla, a handful of betel leaves, usually enclosing a money present.

Cabook, a species of stone, laterite.

Chalia, a caste mainly employed in collecting cinnamon.

Dagoba, a shrine of brickwork erected over a relic.

Devalaya, the temple of a Hindu deity worshiped among the Buddhists.

Disawani, a Province administered by a Disawa.

Dugganna Rala, a courtier.

Duraroba, an imposition levied on cinnamon for the benefit of the Duraya.

Duraya, the headman of the Chaliya.

Esela, the month of July—August.

Etbandana Rala, the Chief of the Elephant Hunt.

Factory, a store where goods were collected for purposes of trade.

Gabadagama, a Royal village.

Gaja Nayaka, the Master of the Elephants.

Gane Bandar, same as Maha Nayaka.

Goigama, the chief caste among the Sinhalese.

Gowwa, a Sinhalese measure of distance, about four miles.

Hena, land under forest and cleared for cultivation at long intervals.

Huwandiram, an imposition similar to the Duraroba.

Kadawatu, thorn gates used for closing and guarding the public thoroughfares.

Karanduwa, a bell-shaped receptacle for a relic.

Karti Mangalaya, a religious festival held in honour of the War God.

Kitul, a palm with strong timber, *Caryota Urens.*

Kodituwakku, small cannon which could be transported by a couple of men.

Kraals, an enclosure formed of beams for capturing Elephants.

Lacham, a Tamil dry measure, used like an amunam as a superficial measure as well.

Laryn, a coin of Persian origin, formed of a silver bar bent into the shape of a hook.

Lewaya, a salt pan in the Southern Coast.

Madapally, a Tamil caste.

Maduwa, a structure in the nature of large shed.

Magul Poruwa, the ornamental platform on which the marriage ceremony is performed.

Maha Nayaka, the Chief High Priest.

Maligawa, lit. a structure consisting of several stories. This is the usual name given to the Temple of the Tooth.

Mohottiar, Mohottala, a Secretary.

Mohundiram, a Military Officer. The word is probably not of Sinhalese origin. It is frequently applied as an honorific to silversmiths and Malays.

Morgen, a Dutch measure of area containing about 2$\frac{1}{9}$acres.

Mudaliyar, chief military officer commanding the Hewayo or Sinhalese militia, who were named Lascarins by the Europeans. Twenty five Lascarins formed a *Ranchu* under an Arachchi.

Mukkuwa, a fisher caste of Tamil origin.

Muttettu, lands belonging to the lord of a village.

Nalalpata, the metal band which was secured to the forehead in confering rank.

Paravas, a caste of Fishermen from Southern India, who were employed as divers at the Pearl fishery.

Patangatyn, a term usually employed for the headmen of the Parava and similar castes.

Pehidun, uncooked provisions supplied as Rajakariya.

Perahera, the chief religious festival of the Sinhalese, so called from the processions which were an essential portion of the celebration.

Pinda patika, one who subsists on the food he begs from door to door.

Plakaat, a legislative enactment.

Polaya, a tax levied on coconut palms.

Rala, an honorific applied to men of high birth.

Ranchu, a band of about twenty five Lascarins under an Arachchi.

Ran Doliya, the Royal Consort of a King, as opposed to the Yakada Doliya, a Goigama Junior Queen.

Rata Sabha, a Council of the leading men of a Rata.

Samanera, an unordained Buddhist monk.

Sannas, a Royal grant.

Sulu Disawa, a sub Disawa, over an inferior Province.

Tanayama, a house used as a resting place on a journey.

Tavalam, cattle employed to convey loads on their backs.

Tombo, a Register, of lands and of men.

Upasamadawa, the Buddhist Ordination.

Veddahs, probably the aborigines of Ceylon, a race similar to the Bushmen of Australia.

Vidane, a supervising officer ; there were various grades of such.

Wanni, the wild region lying approximately between Anuradhapura and the Jaffna Peninsula. It was in charge of semi-independent chiefs called Wanniyas, (Wanichchi, feminine.)

Wasala, the residence of the King, sometimes applied to the residence of lesser officials.

Watu Badda, a tax levied on planted lands.

Wellala, the chief caste among the Tamils of Jaffna.

Yakdessa, one reputed to have certain magical powers ; usually a lay priest at a Devalaya.

CHAPTER I.

The curtain which had fallen on the last crowded scene in the mediaeval melodrama was raised again to show the interior of a business establishment which the Hollanders were employed in reducing into some semblance of order. A conspiracy against them was discovered at Jaffna and fourteen of the alleged ringleaders were sentenced to death. It was considered necessary to strike terror into the hearts of the disaffected, and horrible punishments were inflicted on the condemned men; three of them were stretched out on wooden crosses laid on the ground, and after being stabbed in the neck and breast, were disembowelled; their hearts were then taken out and laid on their mouths, after which their heads were cut off and exposed in the market-place. A Jesuit was beheaded and eleven others were hanged, their bodies being left to rot on the gibbets. A resolution was passed by the Council placing on record an expression of gratitude to Almighty God for the success obtained over the Portuguese, and the 20th of November, 1658, was fixed as a special day of thanksgiving and of supplication for His further aid: anyone failing to observe this order became liable to a fine of a hundred rix-dollars.

The territory of which the Netherlands East India Company now found itself master in the South of Ceylon extended from the Maha Oya to the Walawe Ganga, thus including the entire Matara Disawani, and the most valuable portions of the Disawanis of Sabaragamuwa, the Four Korales and the Seven Korales, which at one time had been administered directly from Kotte. In land its frontiers were marked by the forts of Sitawaka, Anguruwatota and Katuwana. In the North the entire kingdom of Jaffnapatnam, including Manar and extending vaguely to the frontiers of Trincomalee, acknowledged its authority, which however was but lightly felt in the Wanni. The Bentara River served to divide the Sinhalese districts, the Nothern portion being entrusted to a Disawa stationed at Hulftsdorp, outside the fort of Colombo, and the Southern to a Commandeur at Galle, to whom the Disawa of Matara was subordinate. There was a Commandeur at Jaffna; he took precedence immediately after the Governor, who lived at Colombo; this latter was appointed by the Supreme Government at Batavia, and was assisted by a Political Council of the highest officials in the Country. Executive functions were carried out by a Civil Service of six classes, distinguished by trade names such as Merchant and Under Merchant. Boards were organised for the administration of justice and the spread of education and of the Christian religion among the people of the country; while orphanages and poorhouses were started for the benefit of the needy among the Hollanders themselves.

The principles, if such they could be called, which had guided the Portuguese in the mismanagement of the occupied territories, were never accepted by the methodical Teuton. The Company had succeeded to an estate, badly neglected and run to weed, it was true, but with great possibilities and latent resources; these were now going to be developed with patient husbandry and a reasonable consideration for the well-being of the native inhabitants.

Matters were indeed in a deplorable condition. From Negombo to the Walawe Ganga the country was largely waste and unpopulated; the rich tracts of rice fields were lying abandoned, with their dams and water channels destroyed, and the great reservoirs were breached and useless. Thick tropical forest covered many a happy village which in 1505 Lourenco de Almeyda had eagerly scanned from his vessel. Even the Southern coast-road was so infested with wild elephants as to be dangerous to the traveller, and on a generous estimate the population did not exceed 350,000, though the Galle District was in this respect somewhat better than Colombo. At the same time the population of Jaffna was calculated at 120,000 souls.

It was of the first importance that the country should pay its way and not be a drain on the resources of the Company, and energetic steps were taken to secure this object. The supply of food had to be increased, and therefore the Company began cultivating rice on its own account. Several thousand Tamil slaves were imported from South India, and after being branded with the Company's mark were set to reclaim the rice fields; even the work of fortifying Colombo was considered secondary to this urgent question. Poverty and debt had so seriously affected the villagers that large numbers had been obliged to sell themselves into slavery; a regulation was accordingly passed forbidding the purchase or taking in mortgage of the last property of any person, which was essential to his maintenance. Instructions were given for repairing Kattakarai, the tank which had once fed the wealthy province of Mantota, and which like so many hundreds of others was now lying in a ruined condition; its extent was so immense that it was named the Giants Tank by the Hollanders, who anticipated that the lands which its water could irrigate alone would be sufficient to feed the entire North. The sluices of the Musali river had to be kept in proper order further to conserve the supply of water, and the Tamils of the Peninsula induced, in spite of their strong prejudices, to settle as cultivators in Punaryn. The numerous wells which have always formed so striking a feature of the dry Tamil kingdom, were to be attended to, and the cattle which had been killed off by disease and the demands of the European soldiery, replaced by importations from India.

Other industries also were taken in hand; silk worms were introduced from Bengal, and an attempt was made to start the systematic cultivation of the indigo which was found wild in some parts of the country. Cotton growing was encouraged and weavers and dyers enticed over from the Choromandel Coast, in order to compete with the trade which formed such an important source of revenue there. Heavy duties were imposed on imported tobacco, in order to protect the home industry; while a local mint issued in reasonable abundance a copper coinage which, though of the crudest execution yet seen in Ceylon, removed one of the main difficulties in the way of trade. Success, however, could hardly be expected unless the hearty co-operation of the natives of the country were assured. It was of the greatest importance that justice should be carefully administered, and the mind of the Teuton had an instinctive respect for law. The Digest of the Plakaats and Ordinances which Maetsuycker, who since leaving Galle had risen to be Governor General, had prepared under the name of the Statutes of Batavia, was introduced, but experienced Sinhalese invariably occupied seats on the Land Raad Courts, which were mainly engaged in deciding land disputes, in order to see that all ancient customs were observed. The Disawa continued to exercise a summary and paternal jurisdiction in respect of smaller matters.

In the North the Portuguese officers were replaced by Tamils, four Mudaliyars being placed over the four Provinces of the Peninsula. Special consideration was shown to the mild and obsequious Wellalas, and no undue haste was to be employed in forcing a new religion upon them.

The Christianity which the Portuguese had left behind was very nominal in character and consisted of little more than the capacity to say a few prayers, and to make the sign of the cross; indeed several Christians had already applied for permission to resume their Hindu practices. Religious instruction therefore was to be given to all and children compelled to attend school, preparatory to their being received into the Reformed Church. Everyone was obliged to attend Church service, and listen to the lengthy sermons of the energetic Philip Baldaeus and his fellow workers, absentees being punished with fines which were used to pay the schoolmasters. The results of these attempts at conversion were soon reported to be as gratifying as the Portuguese had found them. The *Thesawalamai,* or the custom of the Tamil country, was retained as the basis for legal decision so long as it appeared to be consonant with reason, all deficiencies being supplied from the Dutch Law. At the same time the practice of child marriage was discouraged: the daughters of the Hollanders themselves did not marry till they were twelve or thirteen years of age.

There were about two thousand Sinhalese lascarins on the rolls and all of these were provided for their maintenance with *Badawedili* lands, now called *Accommodessan.* These men still continued under the orders of the Disawa, Pierre du Pon being the first to be appointed to that position in Colombo. The duties of the Disawa were of the most varied kind; he was responsible for the military outside the fort, for the maintenance of roads and the draining of swamps, for the development of agriculture, and for the general well-being of his district. He was also expected to see that prayers were said at the outstations every morning and evening by a well conducted junior officer. Even petty matters of detail were the subject of regulation : the prices of foodstuffs were fixed, and overseers appointed to supervise the bazaars and markets. Only pious men who regularly attended divine service were to be licensed as bakers.

The necessity for the proper maintenance of its own people was not ignored by the Company. The burgher class, representing the free European settlers not in the Company's service, was to be recruited as much as possible from them; they were provided with liberal grants of land with the right of free trade throughout the settlements; and where possible they were preferred to natives for appointment to office.

The privilege of keeping shops was confined to them to the exclusion of their energetic rivals the Moors, whose further settlement in the country was forbidden. Those Moors who had resided in the country for a long time were permitted to continue there, but their occupations were restricted to agriculture and navigation. At the same time the Indian Moors were encouraged to visit the ports of the Island with their merchandise.

The frequency with which the Company's soldiers were marrying native women was a cause of some anxiety; it was therefore resolved that such marriages should not be permitted unless a clergyman was prepared to certify that the proposed bride professed the Christian religion. Those wives were compelled to attend religious service once a week, under penalty of their husbands' wages being forfeited, and the daughters born of such marriages were to be carefully looked after in order to supply wives to the next generation. Great difficulty was experienced in keeping the Teuton sober, and an attempt was made to brew a mild and wholesome beer from paddy. "This seems to be a necessary measure" wrote Van Goens "because we find—God help us—that our men cannot be made to avoid drink."

But above everything peace was essential for successfully carrying out the new scheme of administration, and to obtain peace the Company was ready to pay almost any price. The strength of the army was fixed at 2000 Europeans in addition to the native levies, strict discipline was maintained, instructions were given for the strengthening of all the fortresses, and a careful watch was kept on the frontiers. The Wannia chiefs received special treatment; the Portuguese had been content to leave them unmolested in their wilds on condition of their paying a tribute of a fixed number of elephants every year in lieu of the tythes and taxes which were levied from the rest of the inhabitants in the North; it was found convenient to continue this policy till a suitable opportunity for their complete reduction presented itself. The Company was afraid that any strict measures would induce them to throw themselves into the hands of the King, whereas they could be utilised to act as spies on the Sinhalese, chiefly by means of the *tavalam* drivers who maintained an active trade between the King's dominions and Jaffna. They were however not all equally complacent; and the principal of them, Kaila Wannia of Panangaman, could not be persuaded to accept Van Goens' summons to appear before him; the policy which consequently was adopted was the favourite one of breeding jealousy against him among the remaining Wannias. Directions also were given that the Veddahs who lived on the boundaries of the Wanni were to be treated kindly, in case of future emergencies.

The one incalculable factor was the temper of the King, who was still raging like a caged tiger. He had vowed never again to trust the word of the merchants who had outwitted him, and yet he was grateful to the men who had driven away the Portuguese who had ruined his country. He therefore had not only remained passive during the last struggle in Jaffna, but he even wrote to Van Goens in November 1658 to express his great appreciation of the latter's services. He was no longer the King only of the *Kanda Uda Rata*, the Country above the Mountains, but of the *Sinhale*, the Country of the Sinhalese, including nearly a moiety of the *Pata Rata* or Low Country which had belonged to Kotte. His subjects were in a pitiable condition. Their poverty was so abject that infanticide was of shocking frequency. The stringency with which the King's prohibition of all trade with the Company was en-forced had limited their foreign intercourse to the ports of Puttalam and Kottiar, and they were unable any longer to depend on that barter which had been the means of providing them with so many of their wants. Their hardships were accentuated when in May 1659 a Dutch garrison was placed in the old Portuguese Church at Kalpitiya, this controlling the Puttalam trade. Dense forests had been allowed to grow up not only on his frontiers but they separated the various provinces, and the only means of communication with the outside world consisted of narrow passages which were strictly guarded and closed by thick thorn gates called *Kadawatu*. There was much discontent among the people and the King realised that his popularity was on the wane. He was, however, too engrossed in nursing his own grievances to be regardful of the well-being of his subjects. A plot to poison him which had been recently discovered and punished with terrible severity, made him suspicious of every one, and any subject whose influence, wealth, or success attracted his attention, was removed out of the way without hesitation.

The policy adopted by the Hollanders was to keep him in good humour at all costs, and their attitude towards him was deferential to the point of servility. Repeated embassies were sent to him with presents of rare animals and similar curiosities which he was known to appreciate, but none of these ambassadors would the King allow to return. His hobby was to collect a perfect menagerie of the various European races which visited his dominions. In this way he had got together a large number of Portuguese, Hollanders, and English, among the last being that Robert Knox who was taken prisoner at Kottiar in 1660, and the fruit of whose long detention is preserved in what is perhaps the most valuable account of the life of the Sinhalese people yet written by a foreigner.

The Hollanders had reason to be nervous, for the cloud which was destined finally to overcast their domination had already reached the shores of Ceylon. For the last twenty years the vessels of the British and Danes had been not unfamiliar sights at the harbour of Kottiar, which afforded facilities for repairing them such as were not to be found in any Indian harbour. The visitors had been well treated by the Sinhalese and permitted freely to travel inland, so that they obtained an opportunity of learning the condition of the country. As early as 1658 the Directors of the British Company in London had received a lettter from one of their officers advising them of the desirability of setting up a factory at Kalpitiya, so as to secure a share in the trade of the Island, and matters received a great impetus from the Treaty of June 1661, regulating the conditions for the marriage of Charles II with the Portuguese Infanta. It was there laid down that if either of the contracting parties succeeded in obtaining possession of the Island, Colombo was to be given to Portugal and Galle to England, while the cinnamon trade was to be divided between the two. The same year the British Directors gave orders for the despatch of an embassy to Raja Sinha to obtain permission for build ing a factory and to secure a share in the cinnamon trade, and these advances were received not unfavourably by the King.

The Hollanders were greatly excited by these proceedings. A force was sent to Kottiar but soon returned in consequence of an outbreak of sickness; and steps were also taken to fortify Point Pedro. Don Joan de Costa, who was their chief adviser in respect to occurrences at the Sinhalese Court, insisted that the English and Portuguese were acting there in concert, and that an attack on the eastern Coast or on Manar, was to the anticipated. Sir Edward Winter, the British Agent at Madras, announced plainly what the intentions of his Company were, and was warned that in consequence of the existing arrangements between the Hollanders and the King, any intrusion would be regarded as an unfriendly act.

However, both nations were anxious to cajole the King into releasing his European prisoners, and their ambassadors appeared at Court in 1664. The King was at Nilambe, where he now resided during long intervals at a time for the sake of his health. He had roused the dissatisfaction of his people to a dangerous pitch by preventing the celebration of their greatest festival, the *Perahera,* this year, but the Europeans found him in a more complacent mood than usual. The English prisoners were collected from the various parts of the country where they were lodged and informed that the King was pleased to set them free, and then they were invited to enter his service. They hesitated and were allowed till the next morning to come to a final decision.

In the meantime, a plot had been brewing to kill the King and place his son on the throne. A terrific comet which had appeared in the heavens for some days, filled the minds of all men with gloomy forebodings. On the night of the 21st of December, on which day the prisoners had been set at liberty, two hundred armed men assembled at Nilambe and attacked the guards who watched outside the palace gates; the majority of these were killed before they could recover from their surprise, while a few escaped within and joined the King.

The conspirators followed and occupied the palace, the King with a handful of men being brought to bay behind a wall. The old warrior had not forgotten how to handle the steel, and the majesty of his semi-divine royalty overawed the malcontents who could not summon up sufficient courage to storm the place. The consequence was that on the following morning the King, guarded by his men, sallied out, and driving elephants in front of them to crush down the jungle, escaped to the stronghold of Galauda behind Hanguranketa, fifteen miles away. The houses of the King's partisans were quickly plundered by the English, and then the bulk of the rioters, whose numbers had considerably increased, hurried to Senkadagala, where the Prince was living with the Queen; they took with them the English, whom they in turn attempted to win over to their side, though equally without success.

The rebels now declared Raja Sinha deposed from the throne on the ground of misgovernment. They charged him with gross breaches of the law of nations in detaining the ambassadors of foreign governments and arresting such of their subjects as came to his country. They declared that his vindictive policy had destroyed the trade of his subjects, while his cruelty was a source of peril to the life of everyone. They accordingly proclaimed the prince as King in his room. The latter, however showed no enthusiasm for this unwelcome honour. The 25th was fixed for advancing on Hanguranketa to capture the fugitive, but in the meantime the prince, accompanied by the favourite sister of Raja Sinha, escaped to the King. There was consternation among the rebels. Some fled home in a panic and in such haste that the courtyards of the palace were strewn with the coin which they had brought with them and which the English hurried to pick up. Others fell to quarrelling among themselves; while one great chief declared for the King and seized on the Capital in his name. It was noted with awe that on the night of the 21st the tail of the comet had turned in the contrary direction.

The rebellion was over and the King found no difficulty in resuming control of the government. The rebels had to pay a terrible price for their rashness, torture and confiscation of property being not the least of the penalties with were freely employed. Several priests who were suspected of complicity and who belonged to some of the best families in the country, were executed and their bodies cast into the river. The Prince disappeared, and for many years to come neither the Hollanders nor his father's subjects could ascertain what had happened to him.

The able but domineering van Goens, who as High Commissioner had not been able for some time to work in harmony with the sedate van der Meyden and who had been obliged to suggest to the authorities at Batavia that the Governor was finding the weight of administration too heavy for his years, was himself appointed to succeed the latter in September 1662. The trouble among the Sinhalese was viewed by the Hollanders with unmixed satisfaction, especially as war had broken out between the United Provinces and England. Indeed their Excellencies at Batavia wrote and expressed the pious opinion that the Sinhalese rebellion was "a gift from heaven."

The King in his general distrust of his own subjects threw himself into their arms. At his request a force of Hollanders was despatched into Sabaragamuwa, and occupied a large portion of this District as well as of the Three and Four Korales, while a fort was built at Ruwanella and the Portuguese church at Sabaragamuwa was fortified. In September 1665 du Pon hastened to Trincomalee on the rumour that the British proposed to seize the place, and built another fort there. The Batavian authorities hesitated, for an extension of territory did not suit their policy; but they were overborne by the insistence of van Goens, and acquiesced in what was being done, the more so as it was urged that the occupation of Ruwanella would divert a good deal of the arecanut trade from Kalpitiya to Colombo. They further agreed that Kalpitiya and Negombo should be properly fortified, and Chilaw, which was still in the hands of the King, should be seized. At the same time some small duties on arecanut were given over to the King, in order to keep him in his present complacent mood.

The Company's affairs could at this time be regarded as prosperous. Its first pearl fishery was conducted by van der Laan in 1666, when 400 boats took part. It was calculated that a crowd of 200,000 people was attracted to the scene, and as all the water had to be obtained from one tank, this was soon contaminated and sickness broke out, 1500 men dying in six weeks. In July of the same year the capture of ninety six elephants at one kraal added a considerable sum to the revenue, while its attempts to increase the cultivation of rice had been amply rewarded. Indeed the grain was so plentiful as to cause anxiety that the vessels which imported it from India and which on the return voyage took away the elephants, might be discouraged from coming to Ceylon, and it was therefore decided to leave the cultivation more and more in private hands.

The condition of affairs among the British at Madras was also such as to give the Hollanders satisfaction, for in 1665 Winter with the assistance of the military had turned his successor out of office and usurped the chief control; as this state of things continued till 1669, internal troubles prevented the British from interfering with the Company in Ceylon. Some awkwardness however was caused by the discovery that in 1667 the King had sent envoys to Madras. These men were seized and brought back by the Hollanders, but about the same time a letter was received by the King from Francois Carron, the conqueror of Negombo in 1643. He had now joined the French and been appointed Director of the powerful French East India Company which was started in 1664 with the assistance of Louis xiv. The Company proposed to establish a settlement in Ceylon, and Carron now wrote to inform Raja Sinha that Louis intended at an early date to send to him a nobleman with presents. This no doubt tended to elate the King, who at the same time was annoyed by the cautious advance of the Hollanders to Arandora, the scene of so much fighting in Portuguese times, which they occupied with a garrison. A large force of Sinhalese was soon facing them and watching their movements, while in October 1668 the Sinhalese drove the Hollanders away from the more remote districts of the Sabaragamuwa Disawani.

The Company however was anxious about being implicated in hostilities, for though the war with the English was over, they were having much trouble with the native potentates in South India. One of these, the great Nayaker of Madura, had as early as 1644 given them permission to erect a factory at Kayalpattanam, and when fourteen years later Tutucorin was captured from the Portuguese, the Company succeeded to the rights of the latter over what were known as the Seven Ports, the Pearl and Chank fisheries of Tutucorin, and the control of the Christian Parawas who supplied the divers. A treaty concluded in 1660 between the Nayaker and Van der Meyden confirmed the rights thus acquired by the Company, while at the same time emphasising the liability of the Parawas of the Fishery Coast to pay the same dues to the Nayaker's Government as they had been accustomed to do under the Portuguese. Ramnad formed the Southern portion of the Madura Coast and was ruled by the Thever, a feudatory of the Nayaker, and Guardian of the holy temple of Rameswaram. A separate peace, drawn up on a plate of copper, was entered into with him.

All these interests in South India were administered by the Governor in Ceylon, and van Goens was anxious to convert the Parawas into the Reformed church. The stoutest opposition was raised by the Roman Catholic clergy, and consequently numbers of them were banished from the sphere of the Company's influence. The Nayaker's Regent was not in sympathy with the Company's policy and sheltered the priests, who established themselves among the neighbouring heathen and continued to exercise their old influence over the Parawas, who were at the same time much harassed by the Nayaker's agents. Heavy impositions were laid on them; but the Company, though it found its trade seriously hampered, was afraid to assert itself, and was forced to have recourse to bribes and entreaties to secure the right to do the pettiest things. Its servants were prevented by the Nayaker's Maniagar or renter of the revenue from cutting firewood for its use; its letters were frequently intercepted: carpenters were forbidden to work at its vessels : the repairs to its factory at Tutucorin were stopped: extra duty was demanded on cattle shipped for Colombo: and the cloth-weaving industry which had been carefully fostered, was hampered by the levy of extraordinary duties from the weavers.

At a time when the fleet of Holland was burning King Charles' navy at Chatham, the Company was prepared to see its chief Resident, Hendrik van Rheede, compelled to pay tribute, its judges flogged and fined by the Maniagar, and Hollanders chastised for presuming to ride on horse back. It made an attempt to buy off the authorities, but van Rheede, who was sent with an expensive present, was treated with the utmost contumely. Several members of his mission were beaten, the

Company's flag was dragged in the mud, no answer at all was vouchsafed to the letter which he had brought, and no farewell audience was accorded to the envoy. The submissive attitude of the Company increased the arrogance of the Maniagar, and after the Fishery of 1668 the Chief Patangatyn of Manar was arrested, beaten and deprived of his money. The Tutucorin wells were placed under guard and the Hollanders and Christians prevented from taking water from them. One Hollander who was bold enough to attempt to do so was dragged before the Maniagar and forced to render obeisance to him on his knees. Even an endeavour to plant a hedge round the Company's premises was imperiously stopped. The result was that before very long trade had almost disappeared, and the Company become an object of ridicule along the Coast.

The authorities at Colombo however could not be persuaded to take action, but only entreated their agents to comply with every demand; as a consequence new requisitions were made in respect of the fishery and an armed force was brought up to threaten Tutucorin. The divers were alarmed; no fishery could be held in 1669; and at last the Company made up its mind to meet force with force, and commenced hostilities, though with obvious unwillingness.

CHAPTER II.

Raja Sinha, whose Queen was a member of the the Royal Family of Madura, was well informed of what was going on; no doubt he also knew that the English were again struggling for a share in the cinnamon trade and insisting that Kottiar was a free port where they were entitled to purchase the valuable drug. He had little to fear from his subjects, whose spirit was completely crushed, and his attitude towards the Hollanders began to be marked by increasing arrogance. To placate him certain shipping rights at Colombo and Galle were conceded to him, but none the less in October 1670 he attacked and captured the fort at Arandora, the erection of which he had never forgiven, and carried off the entire garrison as prisoners. The Hollanders blustered, insisted on the release of their men, threatened reprisals, and closed the ports of Batticaloa, Kottiar, and Kalpitiya. The King remained unmoved, but when Hendrik Draak who had been sent as ambassador in 1663 and had been detained by him, died, his body escorted by some Hollanders was sent to Colombo with the greatest ceremony for interment. For years no Hollander had dared to venture on an embassy within the King's dominions, but at last a soldier named Henricus van Bystervelt was found willing to undertake the dangerous mission.

Starting from Colombo on the 21st of February 1671, Bystervelt was received by the King's officers at Sitawaka and escorted in procession to Hanguranketa, for the King never returned to Senkadagala after the rebellion. Another plot to poison the King had been recently discovered and the guilty cooks and other palace servants had been impaled, hanged or thrown to the elephants. Raja Sinha was therefore in a friendly mood towards the Hollanders, who on their part were prepared to humour him to the utmost. The Company's letter was carried within the palace by the ambassador on his head in a golden salver, and he greeted the King with the humble prostrations which eastern etiquette exacted from a King's subjects. His reception was most cordial. The King was warm in his expressions of esteem for the Hollanders, and promised to restore the prisoners he had recently captured and also to send back the previous ambassadors who were being detained by him. He however complained of the closing of the ports, and Bystervelt hastened to re-assure him with the old formula that all that had been done for the better protection of his Kingdom, as well as to punish those traitors to the King who were responsible for the recent acts of hostility.

Bystervelt was appointed a Mohottiar of the King, and presented with the silver inkstand, hour-glass, style and knife which were usually issued to such officers. A sword, a chain of gold, rings and other jewels were also given to him, and so far did Bystervelt's obsequiousness proceed that he carried the set of Sinhalese clothes which was sent to him, within his quarters on his own head. Food was supplied to him daily from the royal kitchen, his lodgings were guarded by Udapalata Disawa himself, an officer who was in high favour with the King and who was said to have saved his life during the rebellion, and he was summoned to numerous audiences. But though months passed in this fashion no substantial business was done. It was clear that whatever Raja Sinha's own feelings were, his Council was bitterly hostile to the Hollanders, and did not hesitate in the ambassador's presence to urge a declaration of war on the Company. The King exclaimed that he would never permit that, but a shrewd Dane who had been at Court for twenty-one years, caustically remarked that the Company always employed fine words to the face, but calumny at the back, of people. Bystervelt, whose training had not been that of a diplomat, was beside himself with rage; he declared that if the detained ambassadors were not sent back, the whole Kingdom would be blockaded; he challenged the King's Councillors to single combat, and finally insisted on being given permission to return. He was coldly told that he could do so and was allowed to withdraw; after some more delay he started on his return journey, and when he reached Colombo on the 29th of October, dressed in all the paraphernalia of a Sinhalese official, he received a warm greeting and the hearty congratulations of the Council.

In the meantime a terrible storm had burst upon the United Provinces of Holland, and threatened their very existence. Louis XIV had by a secret Treaty signed at Dover in May 1670 purchased the services of the licentious Charles II who still disgraced the throne of England, and declared war on the Republic; but the Hollanders, led by the youthful William of Orange, faced the peril with the indomitable courage which had always characterised the race in moments of stress. In March 1672 a large French fleet commanded by Admiral de la Haye, with whom was the restless Francois Carron, appeared at Trincomalee, and seized an island at the entrance to the inner harbour. An embassy was then despatched to the Court and was welcomed by Raja Sinha, who presented the entire bay to the French, whereupon the Admiral occupied Kottiar which the Hollanders had abandoned. A fleet of the latter now appeared on the scene, while the King's troops were gathering along the coast. Sickness however broke out among the French, and on the 9th of July de la Haye sailed away, leaving behind a garrison at Kottiar. This before long was compelled to surrender to the Hollanders, while it was with difficulty that his fleet escaped to the Choromandel Coast.

Before leaving de la Haye sent to the Court a fresh ambassador, Count de Lanarolle, a Huguenot nobleman. The choice was not a fortunate one, for the Count, no doubt contrasting the splendour of the greatest Court in Europe with the squalor of that to which he was accredited, bore himself with a degree of hauteur which was not likely to render the path of negociation less rugged. He travelled on horseback all the way from Kottiar, and when he arrived at Hanguranketa he insisted on riding past the palace, in spite of the agitated remonstrances of the Sinhalese courtiers, who were horrified at this breach of etiquette. The King however took no notice of this, and granted an interview. De Lanarolle was escorted to the Palace by night with the usual ceremonial, but he was so annoyed at the delay in ushering him before the King, that he turned on his heel, and returned to his lodgings. The King was enraged and ordered the ambassador and his suite to be chastised in order to teach them the conduct which was becoming in dealing with Oriental Kings. The ambassador was kept in chains for six months, and his suite, nervous as to the consequences of their chief's arrogant temper, begged to be separated from him. They were accordingly taken to the King's service, and three of them were placed in charge of his favourite horse, while the rest were allowed to settle in the town where they made a living, as so many of the Portuguese who were there also did, by distilling arack and opening taverns.

De La Haye never returned, and De Lanarolle was subsequently pardoned by the King, who made him one of his Mohottalas, and had him married to a Sinhalese lady at Court. Their descendants are well known in various parts of the Island.

The Hollanders were much excited by these events. They feared that the peace for which they had striven so arduously would be broken after all, and hurried to strengthen the garrisons of their out-posts. There was some fighting in the South, but Raja Sinha remained quiet till 1675, in April of which year Van Goens handed over his office to his son Rykloff van Goens junior, who was born in Batavia. Four months later a Sinhalese army appeared before the fort which the Company had raised at Bibilegama, and laid it under siege. They succeeded before long in cutting off the garrison from its supply of water, and then collecting a huge pile of faggots which was pushed over nearer threatened to burn down the entire fort. Further resistance was out of the question, and ninety Hollanders and their four guns were taken in triumph to Raja Sinha. The former were treated with every consideration and several attempts were made to persuade their commanding officer to enter the Royal service, while the guns were mounted on richly carved carriages and retained at the palace as trophies of the victory.

In Colombo there was much anxiety, for the Sinhalese were reported to be threatening Ruwanella. Clement Magellian, a Chalia of distinguished courage and unusual ability, who was sent into the Beligal Korale, was deserted by his men during a skirmish and killed, his head being taken as a trophy to the King. This man had been educated by the Portuguese priests, and in 1663 was appointed Maha Vidane over his caste, in succession to Anthony Mendis. He attempted to raise a body of lascarins among his own people but he fell under suspicion of carrying on a treasonable correspondence with the King, and was placed on his trial. He was honourably acquitted and in compensation was made Mudaliyar over all the Chalia Lascarins, while he won so much reputation in the hostilities with the King that he was permited to increase the number of these lascarins to five hundred men; they however failed him in his hour of need. His death was a great loss to the Company.

Tennekon, now Disawa of the Seven Korales, was hovering near Kalpitiya with his men. In the South the Matara Disawani was being menaced from Sabaragamuwa. Batticaloa was said to be in revolt, and Aripo, the possession of which was of such importance for the protection of the Pearl Fishery, was in danger from the restlessness of Kayla Wannia who was acting in concert with Tennekon. Hostilities would undo all the work which the Company had so patiently built up during the years of peace, and the garrisons were hastily withdrawn from the threatened outposts.

A few years before this a mysterious figure had appeared in the Seven Korales; he declared that he had a mission to preach the religion of the Nameless God, to destroy the dewales in the country, and to establish this new religion. The King watched him with saturnine amusement while he enriched himself with the wealth of the dewales, but when it began to be whispered about that he was the son of his late brother Wijayapala, Prince of Matale, he began to exercise a scrutiny over his actions which was disconcerting to the pretender. The latter therefore fled to Colombo, where he was well received and maintained in state at the Company's expense. There by his shrewdness he acquired, under the name of Ambanwela Rala, a reputation as a wizard which has survived up to the present day. The Hollanders considered that the moment was opportune to make use of his great influence among his countrymen, and emissaries were sent into the Seven Korales to distract the King by creating a movement in his favour. At the same time on instructions from Batavia a humble letter was despatched to the King begging him to take back all the districts which had been occupied by the Company since 1665, to release the Hollanders whom he had captured, and to receive the Company once more into his friendship.

This was followed by an ambassador who took with him a live lion, as a subtle compliment to the King, whose name signified the Lion King. Raja Sinha however was not satisfied with the reports brought to him with regard to the appearance of the animal, and would not deign to look at it. The ambassador was detained at a remote village till the lion died, and then he was summoned to Hanguranketa. Months passed without an audience being granted, till at last the ambassador impatient of the long delay attempted to force his way within the palace. He was arrested by the guards at the entrance and on the King's orders was detained at the spot for three days in order to teach him patience, and then released.

The King displayed much sense of humour in his dealings with the Hollanders, and at a latter date sent as a return present for the despised lion a truculent elephant of gigantic size which had been used as an executioner and which had got beyond control. To neglect this gift would have been deemed an insult to the King, and the Company was obliged to obtain two other elephants to attend on it, and undergo all the expense of its maintenance.

These pleasantries did not distract the attention of the King from his determination to make himself as disagreeable as possible. Tennekon was on the borders of the Kalutara district and all the population retired within the King's dominions, while the Company's outposts had to be abandoned. The collection of cinnamon was seriously affected; there had been no pearl fishery for eight years, and the anxious merchants tried to soothe the King by a present of the two finest Persian horses available. Noone however appeared on behalf of the King to receive them, while on the other hand there was good reason to fear that a hostile demonstration was being prepared on the boundaries of the Three Korales. The outposts here were next withdrawn, leaving a garrison at Sitawaka, and shortly after Tennekon appeared in the Siyane Korale threatening Malwana. He had the reputation of being the most able of the King's Generals and it was believed that the King was regarding his abilities with jealousy. At any rate Tennekon entered into a secret correpondence with the Company's officers, and on the 30th October 1673 deserted to Colombo with his family and three hundred of his men. Van Goens was delighted; a ceremonious reception awaited the renegade, a great collar of gold was placed round his neck, and he was given lands for his maintenance till his services could be effectively utilised. The King betrayed no feeling on the subject, and allowed all the traitor's property which became forfeit to the Crown, to rot where it stood.

The following month Ambanwela Rala fled back to the King; he was not considered of much value and was shortly after put to death. The people of the Wanni were still in a restless condition, and when Don Philip, their most influential chief, died, they appointed a successor to his office without any reference to the authorities at Jaffna. Matters appeared so threatening that it was considered necessary to despatch a military expedition to the district, and this display of force was found sufficient to overawe the inhabitants.

It was during these troubled times that the German, Paulus Hermann of Halle, a physician in the Company's service and later Professor of Botany at Leyden, laid the foundation of European Botany in Ceylon by forming the *herbarium* which was afterwards used by Linnaeus. At the same time Grimm, a Swede, was making some study of native medicine and drugs.

Towards the end of 1679 van Goens, who was then only thirty seven years of age, handed over the administration to Laurens Pyl, the experienced Commandeur of Jafanapatnam, and started for India. In spite of the trouble with Raja Sinha and the anxieties of the war with Louis XIV which had been ended in July of the previous year by the Treaty of Nimeguen, Van Goens had been able to make his term of office a financial success. The monopoly of the arecanut trade yielded such abundant profits as to meet the expence of the increased army of 3400 men; cotton goods were imported by the Company alone, and in addition to the direct profits of their sale, there was a large indirect profit arising from their being used as a medium of exchange for obtaining arecanut. The retail trade in cloth was the perquisite of the burghers. Elephants had been plentiful and their sale had attracted both money and rice, in which latter commodity the animals were frequently paid for. The collection of cinnamon had been satisfactory, and the Chalias had been allowed by the King to penetrate in search of the bark into the wilds of the Pitigal Korale without any opposition being raised.

The labour devoted to increasing the local production of rice had been well repaid and Van Goens confidently expressed his opinion that it was beyond doubt that the establishments of Ceylon could be maintained from the profits derived from its own products. The Lascarins had been increased to 5000 and proved of great service during the recent troubles; as a reward they had received some of the best villages and their lands were largely exempt from the duties to which the lands of others were liable. The Company realised that so long as it refused to surrender Colombo to Raja Sinha, it could not expect permanent peace, and its constant policy was to cajole him with presents. However, plans had been carefully formed as to what was to be done in the event of his death. The Hollanders, adopting the route followed by their illfated predecessors the Portuguese, were to occupy Allauwa and Arandora, and seize the Low Country, while at the same time attacking Chilaw by sea. In such an event much was expected from Tennekon and Punchi Appuhami of Wikeliya, another renegade, who had been appointed Disawa of the Ruhuna and of a part of Matara.

When Van Goens set sail for Batavia there went with him Robert Knox, who at last, after a captivity of nineteen years, had succeeded in escaping from the dominions of the King. He was sent by the Company back to England, where he prepared an Historical Narrative of his experiences which make very painful reading. The greed and the violence of the West had crushed the sweetness out of the life of the East. Raja Sinha, the gallant and chivalrous warrior, had degenerated into an embittered and ferocious tyrant, haunted by the consuming desire to punish the obsequious merchants who had cheated him. Every other consideration was subordinated to this passion; he preferred to see his subjects stricken with poverty and devoid of the most ordinary comforts of life, while the arecanuts which might purchase foreign goods for them rotted ungathered under the trees, rather than that the Company should make any profit from his Kingdom.

Frequent plots against him had rendered him merciless, and the life of no prominent subject was safe; cruel tortures were freely employed, impalement was of common occurrence, the elephants which were trained to act as executioners were kept busy and entire families were exterminated for the treason, real or only suspected, of one member. Others again were arrested and kept in jail for years without a word of explanation or charge. His government was absolutely autocratic, and while he rarely acted under the influence of haste or passion, the advice of no councillor would sway him from the course he had marked out for himself. No officer was implicitly trusted and no one knew what commands had been given to another; each served as a spy on the others; but the common people found that any oppression by the King's officers would be swiftly punished, for the King brooked no tyranny save his own.

Hanguranketa was now his permanent residence. The palace precincts, which covered a large extent of ground, were enclosed by a stout clay wall and abutted on the hill which was the place of refuge, where no one dared to venture on penalty of death. The numerous dependents of the palace lived in low thatched buildings within the precincts, where there were also a few storied buildings occupied by the higher officials. The King's own residence was entered by elaborately carved gates; its windows were overlaid with silver and ebony; and within the palace was full of intricate passages crowded with guards who were not permitted to talk to each other. The King's personal guard was composed of Kaffirs, his attendants were pages of the best families, and his kitchen was in charge of women. As a precaution against poisoning all food had to be tasted three hours before it was served to the King, whose diet consisted almost exclusively of vegetables. The King's *Ran Doliya* resided at Senkadagala with a separate establishment, while the *Yakada Doli* lived in villages close to the palace, where no stranger durst enter.

The diversions which had attracted the King in his youth still continued their hold on him. As the Hollanders knew, he loved strange animals, and a black leopard, a white deer and a spotted elephant were in his menagerie. Though he now rarely appeared on horseback, he delighted to watch his horses being ridden. He was fond of elephant sports and spent much time in feeding fishes in the lake which he had constructed. He liked architecture and was always busy with improvements at the palace. He was proud of his armoury and had some beautiful guns of local make, richly inlaid with silver and gold.

In matters of religion he was very tolerant. Though he himself made little profession of Buddhism, there was at Hanguranketa a College of priests including his own uncle, which supervised religious matters. The temple villages were still so numerous as seriously to affect the royal revenues, for such villages were exempt from taxation. There was a strong feeling among the people for their religion and numerous small temples were built on all sides; these were mean buildings usually of clay, and in no way compared in grandeur with the older buildings which had been destroyed. The Indian Fakirs were still in charge of the sacred Peak, and crowds still flocked to worship the Bo tree among the ruins of Anuradhapura. After the rebellion the King never ventured to interfere with the Perahera, though he himself preferred the *Karti Mangalya* which was celebrated in honour of the War God, and he no longer insisted on being addressed as divine. He respected Christianity, though the scandals which grew round the Church of the Portuguese at Senkadagala compelled him to close it. Even the Moors were permitted to have there a mosque which was supported by a small contribution from the public.

The King still loved a stout fighter; he was very partial to Europeans and always endeavoured to enlist them in his service. Francois Vandenburg was given a high military command till he was found guilty of treasonable correspondence, and executed. Richard Varnham was placed in charge of the artillery and alloted several villages for his maintenance. De Lanarolle, as already stated, was made a Mohottala; and an ambassador from the Company was placed in charge of the Kottalbadda, or Artisans Department, and married to a Sinhalese lady. Several Europeans were employed in the palace and there was a special company of European soldiers commanded by a Portuguese and a Hollander. All the European prisoners were fed at the public expence, till their numbers rendered this a serious drain on the resources of the humble villager. The Europeans however found the want of beef a great hardship, and the Jesuit Verghonce, who also was a prisoner among them, encouraged them to kill their neighbours' cows. This priest was fond of food, and would often visit the temples and share with the tom tom beaters and weavers the food which was offered there. It is not surprising that Knox has recorded with much appreciation that on board Van Goens' vessel "every meal he had ten or twelve dishes of meat with variety of wine."

The Portuguese were given many privileges of trade, and opened taverns where the other Europeans would congregate of a Sunday. The weakness of the Hollander was well known and the Sinhalese proverb which Knox has preserved says "Wine is as natural to white men as Milk to children." It is pleasant to note that in spite of the abject poverty of the people, Knox was still able to say "They have none of theire own nation that begg thare, for all releave those of theire owne families." Pyl continued to treat the King in the manner recommended by Van Goens. Successive embassies were sent, both from Colombo and from Batavia, to secure peace and to obtain the release of prisoners, but the King would not grant them audience. Lions, tigers, horses, civet cats, falcons, Persian sheep and rare fowls were offered in order to tempt him into good humour, but none of these had any effect. The peeling of cinnamon was permitted till the whim seized the King to attack and drive away the peelers, when an humble apology from Colombo secured a further precarious permission. There were rumours that armed forces were again on the frontier, and in consequence the outposts were again withdrawn, and the forts of Hanwella and Kalutara strengthened. It was also whispered about that the fierce old tyrant had taken to: opium or to drink. At last in 1684 an ambassador arrived to announce the King's good health, and not long after the messengers of the Company who had been detained so long, made their appearance with numerous presents. However no mention was made of the return of the prisoners, the matter regarding which there was so much anxiety on the part of the Company.

The Sinhalese now resumed possession of some of the Korales which the Company had offered to surrender, as well as of the salt Lewayas in the South, and no resistance was offered to their doing so. Pyl adopted a most conciliatory attitude ; he sent a private communication to the King admitting that the Company had done wrong in retaining Colombo, that the whole Island belonged to the King, and that the Hollanders were there merely for the purpose of assisting him in its defence He even described himself as the King's "faithful and humble Governor," and Colombo as the "King's imperial and invincible castle." The effect was excellent and it was soon perceived that the King, whose health was known to be in a precarious condition, had softened. This impression was strengthened by the arrival in 1686 of his chief High Priest on a visit to Pyl. This dignitary was received with almost royal honours, and so effective were the Governor's powers of persuasion that warm hopes were entertained of a speedy settlement of the question of the prisoners. A beautiful jewelled Medal was presented by Pyl to Navaratna of Matara, the inheritor of a great name, who was the Chief Mudaliyar and Basnayaka of Colombo, as a token of his appreciation of the share which the Basnayaka had taken in the negotiations.

The expectations thus created were not disappointed, and in May, to the great delight of the Hollanders, the King's Adigar, Aswala Rala, appeared with a long train of released prisoners.

In the meantime Hendrik Adriaan Van Rheede who had been appointed High Commissioner for the Indies, had arrived at Nagapatnam, and Pyl went there to meet him. Raja Sinha was suspicious of his having done so without any notice to him, and sent Mattamagoda Chetty to bring him back. Van Rheede was prepared to make numerous concessions and in August Pyl, acting on his directions, offered to the King's ambassadors to restore all the territory occupied since 1665; but they replied that they had no authority from the King to deal with that question.

Raja Sinha, clear headed to the last, realised that his end was not far off. He summoned a Council of his Ministers at Hanguranketa, and led before them a gentle-faced man, whom he introduced as the Prince Mahastana, his son, and heir to the Throne of Lanka. The secret of his existence had been well kept. The Ministers were silent; they were incredulous but dared not display any sign of hesitation. It is said that the terrible Autocrat had to prostrate himself at the feet of his son, and swear allegiance to him as King, before the Ministers recognised him.

On the 10th of December two ambassadors arrived at Colombo to announce that the prince had succeeded to the Sinhalese Throne. A great demonstration of joy followed; the slaves who were in chains were released, and all criminals condemned to death or to be lashed were pardoned. Five days later fresh ambassadors arrived with the news of the death and cremation of Raja Sinha; they also added that his last instructions to his son were to remain on friendly terms with Pyl, who he believed was not an untrustworthy man like the other Hollanders.

On the 23rd of December 1687 the death of the late King was observed at Colombo by a memorial celebration, accompanied with all the funeral pomp so dear to the heart of the Teuton. Long lines of Lascarins, companies of soldiers and sailors with arms reversed and trailing pikes, each company preceded by a field-piece dragged by slaves, and the Governor's guard in armour, went in front of the trumpets and kettledrums which were on horseback. The great standard of the King, smaller standards, his personal banner, led horses covered with black velvet, gilt spurs, gauntlets, dagger, helmet, coat of mail, etc, came next. These were succeeded by a coach drawn by six led horses, all hung with the King's device of the Red Lion on a gold ground, the horse of State, herald in armour, the Sword of Sovereignty, the Crown and the Sceptre. These last were carried on cushions by noblemen and were guarded by halberdiers, and accompanied by lighted flambeaux. Next came the Governor, whose train of six ells in length was borne by a page, with the Sinhalese ambassador by his side. The Political Council, the Ministers, the Council of Justice, and other officials followed, while the burghers and domestics brought up the rear.

This long procession wended its way to the Church where the insignia remained on a table till evening; then they were removed under three vollies of musketry and a royal salute from all the guns in the city and the fort, and escorted back to the Governor's house with the same marks of distinction. After this demonstration of respect to the memory of the King whose death had filled them with exultation, the weary officers were regaled with spirits and wine and allowed to return to their homes.

CHAPTER III.

On the 10th of July 1688 the Maha Mohottiar arrived from the Court to announce that on the 27th of the previous month the new King had girded on the Sword of State; he brought with him a gun of solid gold as a present for the Governor, and he was accompanied by a long train of Hollanders whom, with their wives and children, the King had been pleased to set at liberty. On the 15th following the new King was proclaimed from the balcony of the Council House under the name of Wimala Daham Surya Maha Raja amidst great shouts of "Long live the King"; a display of fire-works completed the festivities.

The re-arrangement of Colombo which had begun in 1656 was now complete, and the original town, now known as the Old City or *Oude stad*, separated from the Castle. The former in the main occupied the Pettah of today, and was divided into twelve squares; in the centre was the graveyard, round two sides of which ran the public market, where anything from a slave to a betel leaf could be purchased. On the east and south the town was strongly defended by ramparts and the lake, which teemed with crocodiles; the only entrance was on the North-east corner, by the Negombo gate, while the adjacent sea shore was used as a fish market. The buildings within the walls were chiefly of Portuguese construction, and the residents included several Europeans with their Sinhalese or Mestico wives. Outside the walls there was thick jungle running in the direction of *Wolvendahl*, the Agoa de Lopo of the Portuguese.

The Castle itself was separated from the Old City by a broad stretch of marshy ground terminating in the moat into which the original outlet of the lake had been converted, and was protected on three sides by the lake, the sea, and the bay respectively. A causeway connected the Castle with the Old City; on the South West ran the road to Galle through the Galle Gate, while the Water Gate led down by twenty steps into the Bay. Within the Castle and facing the Bay was the Governor's house, and close to it was the house reserved for the accommodation of Sinhalese Ambassadors. Most of the officials resided within the walls, though the finest street was curiously enough occupied mainly by Tupasses and Sinhalese. The five bastions of the Castle were of cabook, and a canal ran within the fortifications and alongside the eastern rampart. Vessels were obliged to anchor a couple of miles away in consequence of the sand bar at the entrance to the harbour.

The plans which the Company had formed for a hostile demonstration on the frontiers at the death of Raja Sinha were left in abeyance, for its officials believed that they could obtain all they desired by diplomatic pressure on his inexperienced successor. They assumed the position that all treaty obligations entered into with the late King, as well as the offer made to him to restore the territory occupied since 1665, were no longer binding; but they soon received a rude awakening. Pyl had declared that all the Island belonged to the Sinhalese King, and one of the first acts of Wimala Daham Surya was to send an ambassador with his *Sannas* granting the historic port of Weligama to Navaratna, accompanied by a request that the *Sannas* should be delivered to the Basnayaka before the full Council.

The Councillors were in consternation; they hastened to explain that when they had described the Hollanders as the servants of the King, they did not mean anything more than that they were there to render the King service. It was impossible for the *Sannas* to be regarded as effective; some evil disposed person, they said, must have suggested the granting of the port in order to annoy the Company; and they hinted that as a matter of fact the King was largely in their debt for the services they had rendered against the Portuguese. However after much agitated discussion they agreed to the *Sannas* being formally presented as requested, but at the same time Navaratna was privately instructed to return it to the Political Secretary.

It was soon discovered that the King did not propose to rule autocratically, as his father had done. He apparently had spent his time since 1664 in a temple, and he had the good sense to allow himself to be guided by Ministers, including his Maha Nayaka, who understood the Company much better than he did; and he had also the valuable advice of de Lanarolle. The attitude taken up by the Court was very simple: the ports of Ceylon must be thrown open and the Company must surrender all the territory occupied since 1665, and from this position the Ministers were not prepared to stir.

The Hollanders, acting under the advice of the High Commissioner van Rheede, tried what would today be described as bluff. They had made up their minds that under no circumstances could the trade of Ceylon be thrown open to their rivals. They declared that the King must enter into a fresh treaty with them and the whole question of the occupied territory must be discussed anew. They accordingly submitted the terms which they proposed as the basis of the new treaty, specially reserving for themselves the exclusive and unhampered trade with the Sinhalese Kingdom, as well as the right to collect cinnamon within the King's dominions, subject to the payment to him of a yearly subsidy; they also suggested that the occupied territories should either be held by them as security for their alleged claim against the King, or be transferred to them absolutely in full discharge of all such claims.

However "His Imperial Majesty," as they insisted on addressing Wimala Dharma, was in no hurry; the terms were carefully considered and were not found acceptable. The Ministers denied that the Company was entitled to make any claim against the King's Treasury; he was willing to grant them the required permission for gathering cinnamon, but as to the rest he desired first to see the Governor personally. This did not suit the Company, and a reply was sent that Pyl could not under standing orders leave the Company's lands unless a suitable substitute was available to take his place; but from this date began the custom of sending every year an ambassador to Court with the promised subsidy, in order to receive formal permission for the peelers to enter the Sinhalese Kingdom.

The Hollanders were not feeling comfortable. The people of the Low Country were going in large numbers to Court to receive titles and distinctions from the King, as Suzerain, and even Navaratna had in consequence of his too frequent correspondence with the King's Ministers, become an object of suspicion. In order to avoid unpleasantness they deemed it advisable quietly to evacuate the mountain Korales, as well as the Three Korales, which were nearly devoid of inhabitants. These were taken possession of immediately on behalf of the King.

Religious questions complicated the situation, for the King was devoted to Buddhism, and within the Company's territory there were shrines which commanded the reverence of all Buddhists. Kelaniya had never lost the sanctity which the visit of Gautama Buddha had conferred on it, and crowds still assembled from the King's dominions to worship at Mulgiri Gala. This latter was a superb mountain temple situated not many miles to the North East of Matara; its sanctity dated from the earliest times of the Sinhalese and fresh glamour had been cast round it by the belief which the Europeans entertained that Adam and Eve were buried there.

In 1682 repressive legislation had been passed by Pyl with a view to check heathenism and to encourage Christianity, and in consequence there were nearly 25,000 professing Christians in the Colombo Disawani. The clergy however were fain to admit that their religion was very nominal and that many professed Christianity from worldly motives, to derive advantages from the Christian Government.

What alarmed them above all was the increasing activity of the Buddhists which manifested itself as more and more people who had been driven into the mountains by order of Raja Sinha, began to return to the Pata Rata. Acting it is said on a hint from Colombo, the King even sent a demand for the rebuilding of the dagobas in the Low Country, the return of the temporalities which had belonged to them under the Sinhalese Kings, and freedom of worship to all Sinhalese.

The Company was afraid to interfere with the Buddhists at Kelaniya, for it would not risk the peace it craved for by incurring the displeasure of the powerful Gane Bandar, or *Maha Nayaka.* The clergy were scandalised, for they had great faith in the efficiency of the civil arm in supporting the Church. What, said they, was the use of repressive legislation elsewhere, when Buddhism was allowed unchecked almost within hearing of Colombo? However the civil authorities would not go with them; they would punish professing Christians who took part in heathen worship, but they were not prepared to forbid the exercise of their religion by the heathen. The clergy therefore adopted the policy which had been followed by the Portuguese before them, and converted a *maduwa* which stood close to the ruins of the ancient dagoba at Kelaniya, into a school. This however had no effect in reducing the crowds which attended the festivals, whereupon they urged that a place of Christian worship should be established there, and in 1692 received permission to do so.

Meanwhile the King demanded that all the Company's territory except the coast forts should be returned to him, and repeated attempts were made by vessels flying his flag to sail out of Puttalam. War seemed inevitable and the Hollanders began to argue that their title to what they occupied arose not from contract with the King, but from conquest over the Portuguese, who had received the same under the donation of Dharmapala. They determined to maintain their rights by force if required, and while strengthening their outposts, kept a careful eye on all the highborn Sinhalese within their jurisdiction.

In the meanwhile the annual subsidy was sent to the King, though it was not always that this was accepted, for sometimes the presents were left abandoned on the road. No cinnamon could be collected in 1690, but in the following year after a long interval a pearl fishery, the first of a profitable series, again contributed to swell the Company's chest. Pyl was anxious to return home; nevertheless in deference to the express wishes of the King, he consented to remain in office while the negocia tions dragged on; nothing however came of them, and in February 1692 he handed over the administration to Thomas Van Rhee, who had already seen much service in the Island.

Obsequiousness and tact enabled the new Governor to administer the occupied districts for a period of five years with much less friction than Pyl had experienced. The peeling of cinnamon was freely permitted, and the collection was so large that the surplus left over after providing the yearly fleet with full cargos, was burnt in order to prevent a glut in the market. The Chalias however proved themselves as turbulent as they always had a reputation for being, and the majority of them fled within the King's dominions, complaining of oppression at the hands of their officers. Their work was of the most arduous kind, and even when there was no opposition by the King's subjects, the danger to which they were exposed in collecting the spice in the elephant-haunted forests, was very great.

The King ordered them to go back, but it was necessary to keep them in good humour; they were given a supply of rice, salt and arrack when they started on their collecting round, and each man received in addition a small present when he delivered the amount for which he was liable. The distribution of the presents was celebrated by a fantastic dance by men wearing hideous or grotesque masks, a ceremony still popular in the South. They were further allowed free passage over the ferries, with the right to bring their produce for sale in the town without payment of duty, and to help themselves to the salt at the Lewayas after the Rajakariya was duly performed.

A severe drought which prevailed throughout 1694 and 1695 caused much hardship to the inhabitants, and loss of tythes to the Company. The elphant trade, which was still conducted on the lines laid down by the Sinhalese Kings, was yielding good profits. The elephants which were captured by the Etbandana Rala in the four *kraals* which were maintained in the South, were collected at the Stalls at Matara, which were under the charge of the Gajanayaka, and had to be fed with coconut branches, plantain trees, and grass from the surrounding villages so long as they were kept on the Company's account.

This was a severe tax on the inhabitants, who were greatly rejoiced when a new system was introduced for transporting the animals by sea to Kangesanturai, to be sold at Jaffna along with those captured by means of nooses and pits in the North. The liability to supply the coconut branches was now shared with the Jaffna people; this unfortunately in combination with the drought so affected the trees there, that the export of coconuts ceased, the province could no longer supply the oil which was required for the service of the Company, and the deficiency had to be made good by importation from Malabar.

The areca trade from which the Governor drew heavy perquisites was flourishing, but the evils of the system initiated by the Portuguese still continued. Lands which did not contain a single tree had to supply a fixed quantity at the nominal figure of four *larins* the *amunam* of 24,000 nuts. The deficiency of any one year was carried forward as a balance due for the next, and in a short time the burden became so intolerable that the owners preferred to abandon their lands and flee the country. In addition to this supply the Company purchased all the areca in the market at nine larins, and in some cases insisted on 28,000 nuts being counted for the amunam, the excess of 4,000, known as *Crescentie* nuts, being the Governor's perquisite. There were also certain *Muttetu* gardens belonging to the Company, the crop of which was collected on its account free of cost.

For some time Jaffna had been a source of anxiety. The Tombo prepared in 1646 under the orders of Dom Philippe Mascarenhas had been badly handled and only fragments of it remained. Accordingly a new Tombo was commenced in 1675, and its preparation soon created intense irritation. The people complained that the *lacham*, the unit of land measurement according to which the land tax was assessed, and which is the sixteenth part of an English acre, was computed as four instead of eight sowing measures; that lands which had been exempted from the old Tombo were included in the new; and that a fresh tax had been imposed on the few arecanut trees which their barren soil supported.

The Company was also alarmed at the power the Wellales had acquired as the result of its patronage. Don Philip Changarapillai, the broker of the powerful Indian elephant merchants whose goodwill was of such importance, was the leader of the caste, and so great was his influence that all positions of authority were disposed of according to his wishes. It is true that he came into collision with Pyl when Commandeur, and the latter gave orders that he and all his relatives should be arrested and sent to Colombo in chains. Changarapillai however escaped to Nagapatnam, from where he soon returned with greater authority than ever. Thc Company therefore resorted to the favourite device of patronising another caste, the Madapallys, to counterbalance and serve as a spy on the Wellales, with the result that the latter made common cause with the Wannias, who in their turn were showing themselves more and more restive under the slight control which the Company exercised over them.

The people of Jaffna were liable to provide a large quantity of palmyra timber at a nominal price, and the Commandeur received certain perquisites from its export. The Tamil proverb says that the tree lasts a thousands years in life and a thousand years in death, and the demand for this durable timber was so great that the valuable female trees which alone yielded fruit and also supplied the most toddy and the best timber, were greatly reduced in number, thus seriously threatening the main source of the food supply of the people.

One of the most attractive qualities of the Tamil man of Jaffna has been always his passionate attachment to the soil of his country. Geologically but of recent origin, the surface consists of a thin layer of sand resting on a stratum of coral and limestone. The spots which are marked by any degree of natural fertility are few and eagerly sought after, and no cultivation can be satisfactorily raised till a soil has been artificially created first by breaking up the hard substratum with infinite labour.

The pride of the Wellala always has been his skill as a cultivator. The manner in which he handles his spade differentiates him at once from the hireling. Long before sunrise and long after sunset the best of them may be seen working on the field, while their wives and daughters, so graceful in the perfect draperies and beautiful jewels which they have the good taste to prefer to imported skirts and hats, help to lead the water drawn from the well to every cultivated patch. The wants of the Tamil man are fewer even than those of the Sinhalese, and all his savings are invested in land, and that in his own limited peninsula. The result is that the soil of Jaffna has always commanded an exaggerated and ever-increasing price, and by 1695 it was reported that this had increased fivefold since the expulsion of the Portuguese.

However this craving for land had another side. All through the country there had existed at one time village tanks formed by the native Kings. In every direction there had been roads, for Jaffna by its nature always was and always will be the best roaded portion of Ceylon. Both tanks and roads had been neglected utterly by the Portuguese, and in the case of the tanks at least that neglect has continued up to the present day. The result was that the tanks were gradually filled up and encroached upon by adjoining villagers, while the more influential and powerful inhabitants began to claim them as their private property. Pyl in 1687 had declared that all tanks belonged to the public, but the interests affected, especially those of Changarapillai's family, were too powerful for him, and nothing could be done to remedy the unsatisfactory state of things.

With a sure instinct for what was in harmony with his brilliant sky, the Tamil loved to wear cloths of red; the Company however found that to gratify this taste, the cloth dyers stole the *chaya ver*, or dye root, which was issued to them on account of the Company, and in consequence the wearing of red cloth was forbidden. The drought had affected the supply of rice, and though attempts were made to attract the Bengal Moors who traded in it to Jaffna, these had not been successful and there was much hardship experienced by the people. Over 3500 slaves were imported to assist in developing the rice cultivation of the North, but the local supply always proved unequal to the demand. All these matters created a condition of unrest which led to open rioting in 1696; the position had to be cautiously handled, and Changarapillai's son, for the father was now dead, was mollified by the present of a horse and an umbrella of state, as the chief of the highest caste.

The persistency of the Sinhalese at last found its reward, and in 1696 Kalpitiya and Kottiar were thrown open to the Indian traders, the forts at Batticaloa and Trincomalee being at the same time converted into petty outposts. European vessels however were not permitted in the Company's ports except to take in such a stock of food and water as they might need. The Court was very much gratified, and the gratification was increased when the Company agreed to place a vessel at the King's disposal to fetch a Chapter of priests from Arrakan.

At the death of Raja Sinha things were in a very bad way with the priesthood, and it was declared that there were not to be found in the country five ordained priests of godly life. From the commencement of his reign Wimala Daham Surya, who had erected a new three-storied Maligawa for the Tooth Relic, had invited the Company to assist him in securing the priests who were necessary to re-establish the Maha Vihare succession, just as his great namesake had done at the beginning of the century. At last the arrangements were completed; two embassies were sent, and the second, consisting of five ambassadors, returned in 1697 with two high priests and thirty-four ordinary priests, and an Ordination was solemnly performed at Getambe.

The effect of this reasonable attitude on the part of the Company was soon visible. The most cordial relations were maintained till the death of the King; the peeling of cinnamon was allowed right up to Balane Kanda, the limit of the *Pata Rata*; deserters, whether lascarins or Chalias, were sent back to the coast; and not even the anxiety of the Sinhalese to attract all the trade they could to Puttalam and Kottiar was sufficient to mar the prevailing harmony. The question of a fresh treaty was allowed to sink into oblivion, as matters were found to work to everybody's satisfaction without the sanction of any formal document.

The King hated war with an intense hatred, and fortunately for his people once again after a hundred and fifty years the influence of a peace-loving priesthood was making itself felt in the counsels of his Ministers. Two Adigars, five Maha Disawas and seven Suludisawas, were responsible for the administration of the country. There were seven Mohottiars, who were mainly concerned with matters of revenue. Nominally each Mohottiar was responsible for a regiment of 900 Lascarins officered by Muhandirams, but the reaction after the truculent attitude of Raja Sinha was so great, that military matters were neglected.

The King's guards were armed mainly with pikes, there were barely a thousand men who knew how to use a musket, and there was no one who could manage the cannon which still existed. These last had been increased in number by the guns of a vessel which had been stranded on the Eastern coast. The three hundred tusked elephants of the King were maintained chiefly for ceremonial purposes and were kept distributed among the temples. There was perfect friendliness on the frontiers, and the unhappy Sinhalese could at last thank heaven for the blessings of peace, and obtain for themselves something more than the barest necessities of life.

The King was quite content; he addressed the Governor as one of his *Dugganna Ralas*, and Gerrit de Heere, who succeeded van Rhee in 1697, continued to subscribe himself from "His Majesty's Castle of Colombo". When this Governor died the King sent anxious directions that good care should be taken to protect the interests of the Company, and that all the stations should be guarded till the arrival of a successor.

"The Honourable and Most Esteemed Lords" the Seventeen Directors who managed the affairs of the Company from Europe, had expressed their disapproval of the excessively servile attitude adopted by Pyl, and directed that terms of address unbecoming to Christians should not be employed towards the King, who still described himself as divine; every respect, however, was to be paid to him. This instruction was interpreted in a generous spirit; for instance a ram which was sent as a present to the King was escorted for four miles from Jaffna by the Disawa and other officials, with companies of soldiers and lascarins, after being saluted with three vollies of musketry and thirteen guns from the Castle.

After an experience of fifty years, the Company was obliged to admit that the question of the Administration of Justice, the importance of which was fully recognised by it, had not been satisfactorily answered. This was especially the case in the North, where litigation was the favourite diversion among a people whose intellect, if not broad, was peculiarly keen and subtle, and whose character was marked by a persistency which could not easily be discouraged. Cases which had been disposed of in Portuguese times would be re-opened, and the appearance of a new Commandeur served as an excellent excuse for bringing up his predecessor's decisions in review.

The neglect which had been shown in the preservation of Court records aggravated this unfortunate tendency. The customs prevailing in the country, and which had to be observed in deciding on the rights of parties, were obscure and often unintelligible to the officers who were entrusted with the duty of interpreting them. These men were usually well-intentioned and were probably honest, but the Company's servants were poor Lawyers, and as a rule there were no law-books provided for the use of the Courts. Some form of codification therefore was urgently required. The condition of the Raad Van Justitie at Colombo, which was the highest Court of Appeal in the Island, was little better, and the Statutes of Batavia and the Local Placaats, according to which Justice had to be administered, were not familiar to its members. The irregularities of Proctors in matters of procedure were a cause of complaint even at this time.

It was probably in view of these admitted deficiencies that Cornelis Joan Simons, who was at the time Vice-President of the High Court at Batavia and who had also the advantage of a legal training at one of the Universities of the Netherlands, was appointed Governor. Under his orders a careful register was prepared of the Regulations issued from the Netherlands as well as from Batavia for the administration of justice, and a convenient summary was drawn up of the Placaats; this latter was to be read out in public every year under the supervision of the Fiscal.

At the same time Claas Isaaksz, Disawa of Jaffna, who had thirty-five years experience in Ceylon, was directed by Simons to make a collection of the Customs of the Tamil country, a work at which he was engaged for nearly three years. The collection when completed was referred to twelve Tamil Mudaliyars, all highborn men bearing the Portuguese title of Don, and was then by an order of the 4th of June 1707, adopted as an authoritative statement of the *Thesawalamai* or Customary law of the country. The Collection, with its quaint reminiscences of ancient matriarchal rights and joint family property, its traces of a lofty code of morality where woman was entitled to the first consideration, and it was a point of honour for the son to take on himself the unsecured debts of his deceased father, is full of interest to the student of social customs, and is still observed as the law in matters of inheritance, mortgage, etc. Moreover in 1704 the Seventy Six Rules and Orders which prevailed in Jaffna were collected together and formally declared to be operative.

The peaceful and unexciting reign of Wimala Dharma Surya which had proved such a blessing to the Island, was drawing to a close. To the end he maintained the friendliest relations with the Company, and even wrote to ackowledge the care with which they guarded the shores of Ceylon. Presents of curios from Nuremberg, tea from China, and horses from Persia, served to keep him amused, while his ambassadors were gratified by the four-in-hands which were maintained especially for their conveyance when they visited Colombo, as their residence had been shifted to Wolvendahl from the Castle. The Company's vessels were always at his disposal to convey his messengers to India; thus in 1706 an embassy was sent to fetch a Princess from Madura as a bride for his son, whose own mother came from that country. In May of the next year he went on a pilgrimage to worship the Footprint of the Buddha on Samanala Kanda, offering at the shrine a great parasol of silver; and having thus acquired Merit he peacefully passed away on the fourth of the following month, genuinely lamented by everyone.

CHAPTER IV.

The new King, who assumed the Sword of State the following year under the name of Sri Wira Narendra Sinha, was a boy of seventeen years, regarding whom little was known except that he was said to have a violent temper. The Nayaker of Madura also was an inexperienced minor, while the Thever was a debauched old dotard. Hendrik Becker succeeded Simons at Colombo, and the opportunity was considered favourable for carrying out the instructions which had been received from the Netherlands five years before, once more to close the ports against the Indian trade. This was done, and at the same time permission was obtained from the Thever to place a garrison at Paumben to prevent European vessels from proceeding coastwise by that passage.

Violent opposition was expected from the Court, for the Sinhalese had been reaping much advantage from the trade which had been opened to them; but to the surprise of everyone little notice was taken of this new measure. Harmonious relations were maintained, and Becker was able during the nine years of his administration to devote himself to the re-organisation of the Company's affairs without any interruption.

His previous service in the country had given him a thorough knowledge of the various existing evils which called for reform, and he was determined not to rely on the information of lazy, prejudiced, or dishonest subordinates, but to inquire into every matter personally, and, as he said, to "lift the veil from the subtle mysteries presented before the eyes of rulers by dishonest servants."

Things were in a serious condition, for the canker which had destroyed the rule of the Portuguese had set in among the Company's officers, who had shown themselves too weak to resist the numerous temptations for the illicit acquisition of wealth. Once again arecanut proved the sorest trial, and the officials were found busily employed in trading in this article in competition with the Company. The best arecanut in the market was bought in for them; forestallers waylaid the men from the Sinhalese kingdom who brought the stuff for sale, forced them to sell it at low figures, or harassed them from place to place; vessels calling for arecanut were supplied with what belonged to them, while the property of the Company rotted in the godowns and had to be burnt.

An extensive system of smuggling was at the same time carried on along the coast. The cloth trade, a monopoly from which the Company expected so much, was being ruined by the Small Company which the officials had formed to carry on a rival business. All these malpractices had to be put down with a severe hand. There were grave scandals in the administration of the Colombo Disawani, which had to be thoroughly purified.

The condition of things in connection with the cultivation of rice in the Matara Disawani was even worse. Little of the rice to which the Company was entitled reached the stores; the best of its lands were cultivated for the benefit of the inhabitants and not of the Company, while the powerful Mudaliyars had obtained for themselves immense tracts by way of Badavedili. Lands were being occupied on all sides without any show of title and without any payment of rent. A Hollander who had been appointed Master of the Sowing was perhaps the gratest knave of all, and in addition he was found to be interfering with the effective working of the Elephant Department, which was in charge of Don Simon Wijayawardhana Mudaliyar, a Sinhalese of high character and distinguished abilities.

Becker did not hesitate. The Hollander was dismissed from office. Wijayawardhana was placed in charge of both departments, and the Disawa informed that his own pompous visits to the scene of the Hunt could in future be dispensed with. It was not long before Wijayawardhana was able to prove to the Company how great was the value of those ancient centres of rice cultivation, the Giruwayas and the Batgan ; enough rice was produced to meet the needs of all the establishments in the South, while the revenue obtained from the sale of elephants increased with rapidity.

The salt which was brought as ballast by the dhonies which came to purchase areca supplied the whole of the seaboard save Jaffna ; this trade was taken into the hands of the Company. The collection of cinnamon was improved and the Chalias treated with much indulgence. Not only were strict rules passed to prevent the destruction of cinnamon plants when clearing forest land for cultivation, but the active co-operation of the King was secured, and he issued similar orders regarding the wild cinnamon in his Kingdom, threatening with death anyone who damaged a tree.

In the North the population had increased and new lands been opened up on all sides ; a fresh Tombo was therefore begun so as to include them for taxation, and orders were given to sell off those for which no good title could be proved. Needless to say this was opposed by the entire landed interest. The horse breeding at Neduntivo was made to yield a profit. The dyeing of cloth for exportation to

Europe and Batavia was going on satisfactorily. All unnecessary expenditure was cut down and an Audit established properly to check accounts. The elephants were, with the King's permission, taken overland to Jaffna, whither purchasers were attracted from India by abolishing the system of brokers, and preventing the petty extortions which used to be practised on the strangers. It should be remembered that no purchasers could be found in the Island itself, where an elephant would have been of no use to a private owner. The advantage of being courteous to the men whose money was sought after was not forgotten, and when the sale was concluded the merchants were served with betel and arecanut and sprinkled with rosewater, and presented with spices.

In spite of the failure of the pearl Fishery, for none were held during Becker's administration, the result of his energy was that never before and probably never after, were the profits derived by the Company from the Island so uniformly abundant. The only source of annoyance was the steady influx of the Moors, who in spite of all restrictions continued to make their way and to obtain lands for themselves.

Narendra Sinha was not popular among his subjects, and a plot was set on foot to assassinate him and to place on the throne a certain Pattiye Bandara, who was said to be a member of the Royal Family. The leader of the conspiracy was Kiriwavule Rala, and with him were associated seven other men of high family from various parts of the Kingdom. Rammalaka Rala however received information of what was on foot and warned the King in time, so that when the conspirators burst into his bedroom and plunged their swords into a figure which lay under the sheets, they found they were attacking the trunk of a plantain tree.

The King had slipped out by Udawatu Kele and escaped across the river to Udugoda Dewale. There it is said the Yakdessa whom he consulted prophesied that in seven days success would attend him, whereupon he vowed an offering to the divinity who presided over the shrine, and went and concealed himself in the cave at Poddalgoda in Udasiya Pattuwa. In the meantime the conspirators had been searching all the royal places of refuge till they learnt where the King was concealed, when the eight ringleaders and a hundred and twenty others made their way to the village. The inhabitants however were loyal to the King, and by means of a stratagem arrested all the conspirators, and produced them bound before him. They were all sentenced to death, while Pattiye Bandara was hung up at Talavinna, and shot to death with arrows by Veddahs. The King was not forgetful of his vow, and the Dewale is said to have been rebuilt by him, while Rammalaka was loaded with favours.

Fortunately for the Company, his relations with it were so cordial that not even the mad behaviour of de Bevere, who was sent as Ambassador in 1714, served to break the harmony. This person, who was a Captain in the army, had been received with the utmost graciousness, but considered himself aggrieved at the nature of the presents which were made to him, and behaved with a degree of rudeness which in the time of Raja Sinha would have involved immediate chastisement, if not death. He would not taste the repast which was served to him after his interview with the King, and asked that it should be given to his slaves. Instead of removing the presents with all reverence, he tied them in a bundle at the foot of the palanquin which he had been permitted to use. He abused the courtiers who were sent to escort him, threatened to chastise one of the minor headmen, and outrageously insulted a priest, whose person was regarded as almost sacrosanct. The Company was in consternation when these matters were reported by Gunaratna Mudaliyar who had gone as Interpreter; De Bevere was placed under arrest immediately on his return and an humble apology was conveyed to the Court, which took no further notice of the matter.

Indeed so complacent was the attitude of the King that when in the following year two of the Wannias sent a message to him asking for his protection and assistance against the Company, so far from listening to them he had the messengers arrested and sent with their letter to the officials at Colombo. A small display of military force was found sufficient to quell the threatened disaffection, and the property of the two Wannias was confiscated. It was further discovered that extensive smuggling had been carried on from the Wanni, and a small fort was erected at Mullativo to keep this in check. The following year a special embassy arrived conveying to Becker his appointment as Privy Councillor to the King, as a mark of Narendra Sinha's appreciation of his services. Shortly afterwards he was succeeded in office by Isaac Augustin Rumpf, another member of the local Service.

There were however symptoms that the King was dissatisfied with the restrictions which had been imposed on the trade of his subjects, and the *Kadawatu* which led to the Company's territory were kept closed. The villagers were not prevented from bringing provisions for sale, but the supply of areca was stopped. A formal demand was made for free trade at Puttalam, and a definite answer was returned that in view of the instructions from the Netherlands this could not be permitted. The natural result followed, for the bold Moors of Kilakarai, who were chiefly affected, were not prepared to acquiesce in the arrangements of the Company, and landed on the coast to the north of Kudiramalai.

This was a spot held in great reverence by mariners because of the tomb of a Saint which was there, and had been known to the Greeks under the name ot Hippouros, which is a translation of the native name. It was a convenient centre from which to open communications with the Sinhalese Kingdom. The Company was therefore obliged to strengthen the military guards along the western coast and have a sloop cruising near Aripo. An attempt made on behalf of the King to fish for pearls off Chilaw was forcibly stopped, but the appearance in the neighbourhood of some of the King's officers with a large retinue necessitated a further military demonstration there.

Nevertheless in 1721 Rumpf had the satisfaction of announcing the highest revenue collected by the Company for the hundred years following the capture of Galle in 1640.

For the first time in the century a pearl fishery was held in the following year and this was repeated for the next four years ; no cinnamon however could be collected in 1723 in consequence of another revolt among the Chalias. They complained of the excessive burdens laid on them, refused to proceed to the woods, and applied to the King for protection. The Court was not prepared to support them and Rumpf was able to compel the rebels into submission, and to punish them by depriving them of some of the privileges which had been conceded to them. Rumpf himself died this year and little of interest occurred till Petrus Vuyst undertook the administration in September 1726.

This young man of thirty years was a native of Batavia, being the son of a European father. The three years of his administration recalled the worst days of Dom Jeronymo de Azavedo, and form the blackest page in the history of the Company in Ceylon. The one charitable conclusion is that he was suffering from homicidal mania which developed under the stimulus of his accession to power. The anxiety of the Court to maintain peace increased his opportunity. He began by quarrelling with the civil and military officials, whom he treated in the most imperious fashion; he ended by the infliction of inhuman tortures and murder. At last the authorities at Batavia were moved to a realisation of what was taking place and Stephanus Versluys was sent to replace the madman, who was taken away in chains to stand his trial. A special Tribunal inquired into his case and sentenced him to be beheaded, his body to be quartered and burnt, and the ashes cast into the sea.

Versluys had come out with a special commission to restore order and to render justice to those who had suffered from the actions of Vuyst. Unfortunately he failed to satisfy either the authorities or the inhabitants, and was soon entangled in quarrels with the local officials. A great flood which swept over Jaffna in 1726 had been followed by famine and disease, just as in the time of de Oliveira a hundred years before. There was much suffering among the people everywhere, and this was aggravated by the high price of rice. Versluys was soon recalled, and directed to hand over the government to Diederik Van Domburg, the Commandeur of Galle; instead of doing so he entrusted the administration to the Commandeur of Jaffnapatnam, and Van Domburg found the Castle of Colombo closed against him. He appealed to Batavia, and in December 1732 Jacob Christian Pielat arrived as Commissioner to restore order.

Fortunately relations with the Court continued friendly, though Rammalaka and Hulangomuwa, the two Adigars, were complaining of the closing of the ports. The King was kept in good humour by presents of the same nature as were sent to his grandfather. A carriage and four, camels, and other curious animals from all parts were much appreciated, but not more than the wigs which were sent for the personal use of Narendra Sinha, who had aged prematurely. A great loss befell him when in 1731 the stores at Hanguranketa were burnt down and the treasures of gold and silver which were kept there were destroyed. The King usually resided at Kundasala, a few miles from the Capital, where he had established a charming suburb by the bank of the river, but he maintained his interest in the Capital, where he replaced the Maligawa which his father had erected by a handsome two-storied building.

It was however manifest that the dissatisfaction regarding the closing of the ports was serious, and though the King's own arecanuts were purchased at a higher price than was paid for ordinary nuts, the Kadawatu remained closed; and when Pielat urged the ambassadors who visited Colombo in January 1734, to have them opened, the reply of Dodanwala Rala who headed the embassy and was Disawa of Sabaragamuwa, was, that this could not be done till the trade of Puttalam was free.

This feeling of dissatisfaction spread to the Company's subjects, and even in the neighbourhood of Colombo there were riots, the populace declaring themselves for the King. The unrest was particularly marked in the important Siyane Korale, where military action was found necessary. Several of the rebels fled to Court where they received lands and were allowed to settle down, while those who returned were at the request of the King left unpunished.

The reform of abuses kept Pielat busily employed. A good many of the officials were incompetent, several were dishonest, and the majority hated each other and were glad of an opportunity to ruin their rivals. Several were after inquiry removed from office. A scrutiny of the accounts of the Court of Justice and of the Orphan Board led to the Secretaries being put on their trial for embezzlement, the Secretary of the former avoiding punishment by killing himself in jail.

The proceedings of the Courts were characterised by serious irregularities, delay and negligence. The system of penal law which prevailed, and which was in accordance with the practice in Europe, was appallingly severe. For instance it is recorded that in 1669 an unfortunate Chetty who had been guilty of what today is regarded as merely a social offence, was sentenced to be hanged, his corpse to be put into a sack and cast into the sea. However, this sentence was commuted, and instead, he was flogged under the gallows, branded, and banished for life. In 1751 a woman named Joana, who was found guilty of slave stealing, was strangled by being tied to a pole, her head was then sundered from her body, which latter was dragged to the public place of execution and stretched on the wheel and left there to be devoured by the fowls of the air.

Breaking on the wheel was not customary, and instead it was usual to crush the thigh-bones of criminals with an iron club. As a rule the death sentence was executed by the gallows and not by the sword; an accused person could not be sentenced to death till he confessed his guilt, and the difficulty this created was got over by torturing the man whose guilt was considered proved, till a confession was wrung from him.

The Fiscal who was responsible for the public jail was found to be imprisoning people at the guard-house of the Lascarins on his own authority, inflicting fines on them and proceeding to the extremity of flogging them to enforce payment. Subordinate officials had taken on themselves to sign orders for the issue of supplies from the Company's stores, an authority which was vested in the Governor alone, and the not unnatural result was grave abuse. There was much discontent among the natives of the Colombo Disawani, and it was not all without reason. Tact and patience were required to get matters into order, and Pielat found that there was much work for him to do. He left early in 1734 and Van Domburg took charge of the administration, when the smouldering discontent in the country broke out in a violent conflagration.

The trouble began with a fresh strike among the peelers who had been sent within the Seven Korales; they refused to work unless their grievances against their officers were inquired into and the exactions practised on them abolished. They specially complained of the extra cinnamon they had to collect for their Durayas under the name of *Duraroba* and of the *Huwandiram*. The peelers employed in the Three Korales struck in sympathy with them. The Company appealed to the King to bring his authority to bear on the men, and at the same time tried to appease them by removing the Cinnamon Captain from office. The infection however spread to the peelers in the Galle and Matara districts, and in consequence no collection was possible.

But others besides the peelers had their grievances. The regulations made for the protection of wild cinnamon had interfered seriously with the *chena* cultivation on which the villagers largely depended for food; the fines imposed for non-attendance at School had become a source of oppression; a half of their lands for which no documentary title could be produced had been claimed for the Company and the owners compelled to purchase them at an appraised value; though all coconut trees were liable to the *pol-aya* of a tenth, a further exaction called the *watubadda* had been introduced. Many hard-working villagers were thus converted into vagrants, while the forcible seizure of their cattle to supply food to the officials aroused passionate resentment among people who could not be bribed by money payment to part with them for slaughter.

In a short time the entire country to the North of the Bentara river was in a riotous condition. The coffee garden which the company had opened at Peliyagoda was destroyed, the arrack in the Company's stores was emptied on the ground, and the Lascarins in charge removed as prisoners. A detachment of soldiers was sent in pursuit, and near Malwana shot down several rioters who tried to resist with clubs and knives.

The Council, however, decided that it was necessary to concede nearly all the demands of the rebels, and the Duraroba, Huwandiram, and Watubadda were abolished; but though the bulk of the people returned to their homes, the condition of things in the Siyane, Hewagam and Salpiti Korales which had declared themselves under the protection of the King, was so serious, that an urgent application for three hundred Malay troops was despatched to Batavia. An appeal was also made to the King; but he was not sympathetic, and replied that as the result of his inquiries he had ascertained that the trouble was due entirely to the misrule of the Company's officers.

In the meantime the rebellion, for such it had become, spread into the Galle and Matara districts, and the gravity of the situation was daily increasing. A military force was sent to Attanagalla to over-awe the Siyane Korale, but the rebels, now openly supported by Lewke Rala, the masterful Disawa of the Three and Four Korales, attacked them with such effect that they abandoned their two pieces of cannon and fled precipitately to Malwana. The rebels followed in hot pursuit and they retired to Colombo, being chased by the excited Sinhalese as far as Peliyagoda, three miles from the Castle of Colombo. The Council could think of no better course to adopt than to send an embassy with presents to appease the King. In the midst of all this turmoil Van Domburg, who should never have left his desk at Galle, died in 1736; his successor Gustaaf Willem Baron Van Imhoff, arrived in July, and in the interval the Council at Colombo did what it could to control the situation, at the same time anxiously demanding military assistance from Batavia.

Van Imhoff took matters firmly in hand. The peelers were pacified ; Navaratna Mudaliyar, son of the great Basnayaka, was banished to Tutucorin ; and a disavowal of any sympathy with the rebels was obtained from the King. It is true that the ring-leaders found an asylum within his dominions, but an embassy which was sent to him in 1738 with valuable presents was cordially received. The King however was in poor health, and a Doctor was sent up from Colombo to attend on him ; but early in the following year Narendra Sinha, or Kundasala, as he was popularly known among his subjects, died.

CHAPTER V.

With the death of Narendra Sinha the Sinhalese Dynasty came to an end. Following the custom which Wijayo had commenced, he had obtained his Consort, Udumale Devi, from Madura. She was the daughter of Pitti Nayaker, described as being of the Wadegai caste, and the King had subsequently married her two sisters as well. None of them had borne him an heir, and therefore at his death he nominated their brother, who was known as Hangurnketa from his usual place of residence, to succeed him on the Throne.

This nomination was not acceptable to all; the King had left by his *Yakada Doliya,* a Goigama lady, a son named Unambuwe Bandara, who had at Court a strong following which pressed his claim to the succession. On the other hand there was a feeling of jealousy among some of the courtiers, who feared that the accession of Unambuwa would place too much authority in the hands of his relatives. Matters remained in a state of suspense for nearly a year, and then the wishes of Narendra Sinha prevailed and his brother-in-law assumed the Sword under the name of Sri Wijaya Raja Sinha. Unambuwa, it is pleasant to record, was left unmolested at Court.

The administration of Van Imhoff and his three immediate successors ended with the promotion of the last of them, Julius Valentyn Stein Van Gollenesse, to be Director General at Batavia, whither he started in March 1751. Van Imhoff himself was distinguished by greater breadth of view and liberality of mind than was usual among the men whom the Company selected as its chief representative in Ceylon. He fully realised the value of the Island, and he also realised that ignorance and selfishness had brought the Company into extreme danger.

For the full enjoyment of the advantages which the country afforded, the exclusion of all possible rivals was necessary, but even more necessary was harmonious co-operation with the Court. The authorities at Batavia were not prepared to face the difficulties of the problem, and however much against his wish, he was compelled to have recourse to the tactics of his predecessors and pacify the Court with presents.

It was impossible to believe that the Sinhalese would acquiesce in the existing arrangements much longer. The King received nothing for his cinnamon but an annual subsidy of a few thousand rix-dollars, while his subjects obtained for their arecanuts a sum which barely covered the cost of transport. If on the other hand the King's territory were developed and produced the articles which the Company wished to purchase, both sides would reap the benefit and the Sinhalese would recognise before long that the advantage of the one was the advantage of the other, and that peace was for the benefit of both.

He therefore on every occasion urged this point of view on the courtiers ; he suggested that this would be of greater practical advantage to the King than the opening of the port of Puttalam which they were always pressing for and which the Company had determined to refuse. They were now demanding the restoration of Trincomalee as well, and Van Imhoff was determined to resist this even by force if required. He however recognised with serious concern that all Sinhalese looked up to the King as Lord Paramount, and that it was very easy for him to stir up trouble in the Company's territories whenever it suited his purpose.

In Madura the last of the Nayakers died in 1732, and for many years to come that country was the prey of rival factions and foreign invasions. Finally in 1743 it was occupied on account of the Great Mogul and entrusted to the Nawab of Arcot, who, supported by the English, took up his residence at Trichinopoly.

Shortly after his accession the King married, "for the prosperity and improvement of the world" * a lady from Madura, the daughter of Narenappa Nayaker, who was probably a Polygar or nobleman of that country, and who with several members of his family accompanied the new Queen to Court. There Lewke Rala, a member of one of the leading Pata Rata families of the Four Korales, was the most influential Minister. Another experienced courtier, Mampitiya Rala, who was now in charge of Sabaragamuwa, exercised an influence which was almost as great.

The succession of a Dravidian dynasty did not lessen the interest of the people in their religion, which had suffered under Narendra Sinha, who had been indifferent on the subject. The old scandals had revived, and with worldly prosperity the priests themselves had become worldly. There were bitter complaints that they who were vowed to poverty tried to rival the nobles of the country in their manner of living; that the professed mendicants who should beg for their food from door to door, were ashamed to be seen with their begging bowl. The King sympathised with the popular feeling, and he was warmly supported by his Queen.

A figure which in the depressing mediocrity of Sinhalese life in the eighteenth century, might be considered almost as great, was forthcoming to

* Eheylepola Sannas, Lawrie, p. 200.

direct the popular feeling. This was Saranankara, who was born in 1698 at Weliwita in Tumpane, and had joined the priesthood as a Samanera at the age of sixteen years. In a short time his religious fervour was noised about throughout the country. His life was of the austerest kind, and as he lived on the alms of the charitable he was known as *Pindapatika.* His great eloquence and charm as a preacher drew vast crowds to hear him expound the Dharma; and after he took up his residence at Malwatta Vihare, he became a recognised force in the religious world.

In addition to his reputation as a priest he was the foremost scholar within the Kingdom. The Kanda Uda Rata had contributed little to the fame of Lanka as a centre of learning, and during the early period of the Company's influence in Ceylon, the whole country was nearly as barren of literary fruit as it had been in the Era of the Portuguese. Kirimetiyawe Mantri's Maha Hatane, a fine panegyric of Raja Sinha, was the only writing of merit in the latter half of the seventeenth century, while a prose work in Sinhalese, named the Sara Sangrahaya, appeared in 1708. The Court of Narendra Sinha produced some highflown, Sanskritic, and often erotic poems in honour of the King, but Kundasala's chief claim to remembrance arises from the fact that he had the judgment to patronise the one man who was able to save for his kingdom such fragments of learning as still existed. Saranankara was entrusted by the King with the preparation of several works on religious topics, as well as the translation of a Pali medical work, the *Bhesajja Manjusa.* Round him there gathered a group of earnest scholars and devout men who were destined to leave their mark on the history of their countrymen.

Religious deeds were greatly in fashion. Individuals planted *bo* trees, repaired temples, and dedicated lands for their maintenance. These endowments were placed in the charge of caretakers, who enjoyed their produce subject to the duty of serving the sacred place. Public feeling was the chief protection against neglect and dishonesty on the part of these men, and at the same time the King's officers were expected to deal with any breach of trust, while the village elders would meet and elect a new guardian.

When a new temple was built the most expensive item was the images and painting the walls, which were done by members of the Smith caste. These men would be fed and clothed while engaged at their task, and after the dedication of the temple they were generously rewarded, usually in kind. Their remuneration often included lands and clothes, household fittings and jewels, farm implements and cattle. A *Pin wattoru* or report setting out the nature of the work done was then prepared and submitted to the King, and he would be invited to share in the Merit of the pious work; he frequently expressed his gratification by a substantial addition to the endowments.

With the liberality of mind which characterised Buddhism, Roman Catholic priests had been permitted to enter the Kingdom freely, and to minister to the Portuguese who were settled there. In 1682 the Congregacao of the Oratory of St. Filippe Neri had been started by some Indian Christians at Goa, and was joined shortly after by Joseph Vaz, an Indian and a native of Salsete. About the year 1690 he entered Jaffna as a missionary, and succeeded in making his way from there within the Kingdom. From this centre he organised a Roman Catholic campaign which gave much trouble to the Company, for Vaz was a man of singular decision, energy, and resource, and appeared to be ubiquitous. A Church was built at Bogambra and a few priests collected there to assist Vaz.

Among them was another native of Salsete, Pedro Ferrao, who had a great reputation for sanctity.

It was asserted of him that he once had a personal conflict with the Evil One; at any rate he possessed some of the qualifications which in mediaeval times were considered indicative of piety, for it was extremely rarely that he changed his clothes, and he was as verminous as Thomas à Becket or the Russian Rasputin. The success of these men now began to attract the attention of the Ministers. It was reported that their activities were directed towards the destruction of the religion of the country, and that money was largely employed to secure so-called converts among the poorer classes of the Sinhalese. The result was that the King issued orders for the expulsion of the priests and the destruction of their places of worship, though these orders do not appear to have been strictly enforced.

But the main anxiety was to restore the Buddhist priesthood, and the Company with its policy of humouring the Court, was persuaded to convey an embassy to Pegu to secure a fresh Chapter of priests from there. The deputation started in 1741, but all the members of it except Doranegama Rala perished in consequence of the vessel being wrecked off the Pegu coast.

This complacency however did not go far to assist the Company, for Van Imhoff's successors had not the ability successfully to carry out his policy. Complacency on the one side was met by increasing arrogance on the other. The Dravidians from India fully understood the importance of unhampered trade, and under their influence the Ministers were determined to insist on the removal of all restrictions. Leave was refused to peel cinnamon, raids were carried on along the boundaries of the Colombo Disawani, the work which the Company had commenced at Attanagalla was forcibly stopped, and the erection of a Church in the Hapitigam Korale forbidden.

The Company meekly submitted to all this, with the inevitable result; and a large portion of the Siyane Korale was soon after taken possession of on the King's account. An extensive system of smuggling was organised in co-operation with the Coast Moormen, who boldly conveyed the produce of the King's territory in their boats from the creeks and backwaters between Negombo and Puttalam. An urgent remonstrance addressed to Court was met by the contemptuous reply that the smuggling was very profitable to the King, and that unless the port of Puttalam was opened the Company might find its loss even greater. Armed vessels therefore had to be kept patrolling up and down, but the Moormen were the more experienced in these dangerous waters and little could be achieved in checking their enterprise.

Narenappa Nayaker now appeared on the scene and attempted to take his own vessel by force past Kalpitiya. The refusal to allow him to do so exasperated the haughty Indian, and he vowed that the Company would find him a veritable firebrand. He was as good as his word ; he arrested the Company's officers in the neighbourhood: detained the Gajanayaka who was taking its elephants to Jaffna ; stopped the despatch of provisions to Jaffnapatnam ; and drove away the Lascarins who were placed on guard. Things looked very threatening, for a protest addressed to Court secured no redress ; a company of soldiers was accordingly sent by sea to watch the Nayaker, when the death of the Queen recalled him to Court.

But the troubles did not end, for the Chalias went on strike again and refused to peel. It was well known that this was done at the instigation of the Court, and an appeal was made to Lewke, who supported by Mampitiya and the Udagampahe or Second Adigar, Samanakkodi, headed a faction which was opposed to Ehelapola, the Pallegampahe Adigar ; Lewke was considered to be favourably inclined towards the Company, and the latter did not fail to make it worth his while to continue friendly. None the less incursions were made into the Siyane Korale, the King's Wanniyas plundered the Company's lands at Musali, there was a fresh strike among the peelers, and the messengers who were sent to talk them over were soundly flogged; while in the East the watch houses which the Company maintained near Trincomalee were burnt to the ground.

Nevertheless in 1747 the obsequious Company once again won back the favour of the Court by placing a vessel at the disposal of another religious embassy which was despatched to Siam by way of Batavia. As a result numerous presents were sent to the Governor by the King, who in the same year married a second time. An Ambassador was sent to convey the good wishes of the Company on the occasion; he was received with much kindness, but in the month of August while the Ambassador was still at Court, the King fell ill and died.

When Narenappa Nayaker accompanied his daughter to Court, he brought with him his two sons; the elder of them was now about sixteen years of age and was nominated by the late King, who had no children, as his successor, and the Ministers acquiesced in the recommendation. The administration remained in their hands till 1751, when the new King, whose great physical beauty was a source of delight to his subjects, assumed the Sword with the name of Kirti Sri Raja Sinha.

Lewke still continued in power, and friendly relations were maintained with the Company, which was anxiously watching events in India. There the French and the English were at war, and the English Admiral, Boscawen, opened a confidential correspondence, couched in the most flattering terms, with the Governor, and attempted to persuade him to assist the English Company; but the Hollander was too shrewd to allow himself to be drawn into the fight.

In 1749 the King married the daughter of Nadukattu Sami Nayaker, the bride being conveyed to Ceylon in a vessel belonging to the Company, and with her there came her parents and other relatives who all settled down in Court. The King appreciated the fact that only a Buddhist could be the King of the Sinhalese, and devoted himself enthusiastically to the religion of his people. Though there were no ordained priests available, novices were collected and encouraged, temples were repaired, preaching halls established and religious books copied and distributed. The sacred shrines of antiquity were visited by the King, elephants and horses were offered to the Great Bo, and a festival was celebrated at Mahiyangana. The Esala Perahera which was "regarded by all the people as conducive to prosperity"* was observed with great pomp, the King himself taking part in the procession.

Parakrama Bahu the Great was the model which Kirti Sri set before himself; he visited Polonnaruwa, and came back with the resolution, "I also will walk in the excellent path of the duties of Kings." *

The people were intensely stirred; religion was in the mouth of everyone. Samanta Kuta—Sri Pada, the Sacred Foot Print,—had been taken from the custody of the Priesthood by Raja Sinha of Sitawaka, and entrusted to the Indian Andi, "who rub ashes all over their bodies, thus foreshadowing that they will be reduced to ashes by the fire of the most horrible hell." * The insult had been bitterly felt and never forgiven, and now the King took it back from the Andi and appointed as its custodian the most respected man in his Kingdom, Saranankara. At the same time the great village of Kuttapitiya in the Navadun Korale, once the Nindagama of Simao Pinhao, the doughty Portuguese husband of Raja Sinha's grand daughter, was dedicated to the service of the Foot Print.

The ambassadors sent by the late King in 1747 had reached Batavia, and, leaving behind the presents

* Mahawansa.

they had brought with them, had continued their journey to Siam, to ascertain if the Maha Vihare succession was available there. They returned from their quest only to learn that their King was dead. The Company's officers therefore advised them to take no further action till the wishes of the new King were known, and accordingly they started back home; few of them however lived to see their country, for the majority perished on the voyage.

These repeated misfortunes did not damp the ardour ot the religious party. Ehelapola was the staunch supporter of Saranankara, and as the result of their exertions a fresh mission consisting of five ambassadors and sixty-one attendants, started in August 1750 from Trincomalee with a letter for the King of Siam. After narrowly escaping destruction in a storm they arrived at Batavia where adverse winds compelled them to remain for six months. When at last they reached Siam they were received by the King with the most gratifying kindness, and a vivid account of their experiences has been preserved.

A Chapter of priests headed by Upali Maha Thero accompanied them on their perilous voyage back, and on the night of Saturday the Full Moon day of the month of Esala in the 2299th year after the death of the Buddha, in the presence of the King, Kobbyakaduwe Unanse, Saranankara, and four others were solemnly admitted into the *Upasampadawa.* "And thus after many years this solemnity of the Great Ordination, which so long had been neglected in Lanka, was established once more amidst the rejoicings of the populace, the triumphant noise of drums, chanks, and the five kinds of music, and the roar of cannon."*

Within three years seven hundred priests had been ordained and several thousand youths of good family had entered the temples as Novices. Saranankara was raised to the high dignity of Sangha Raja,

* R. A. S. Cey. Vol, xviii p.--38

or Chief over the entire priesthood, an office which seems to have been in abeyance since the death of Sri Rahula, and placed in charge of the religious establishment of the country. When at length the Siamese priests returned home, the ambassadors who escorted them back took with them a model of the Tooth Relic as a present from the Sinhalese King to the pious King Dharmaka of Siam. The present was gratefully accepted, and a fresh Chapter of priests set out for Ceylon in October 1755. They brought with them, as their predecessors had done, numerous religious books and rich offerings for the Sacred Tooth.

Early in 1751 Lewke died suddenly after returning from an embassy to Colombo, and was succeeded in office by Dumbara Rala. Van Gollenesse left in March, and six months later Joan Gideon Loten arrived as Governor. The policy of peace with the Court was rigidly adhered to and Lienderan de Saram, a *persona grata* with the Ministers, was appointed Maha Mudaliyar, with the name of Karunaratna. He was the nephew of Wijaya Sriwardhana Maha Mudaliyar, who till 1736 had been of great service to the Company in their negociations with the Court. A magnificent jewelled medal was presented to Karunaratna, and its Latin inscription bore evidence not only to the Company's appreciation of his loyalty and zeal, but also to the scholarship of the new Governor, who had some reputation as a student of Natural History.

Loten was not fortunate in the circumstances his administration. Plague broke out in the country and played havoc among the population. This was followed in May 1755 by a cyclone which ruined valuable plantations. In consequence the inland revenue was seriously affected, and there was much restlessness among the people. Moreover there was friction with the Hoofd Administrateur, the official entrusted with the supervision of the Company's Trade and Commerce. He was charged before the Council with neglect of duty and peculation, and there followed a violent scene, embittered by personal recrimination. The accused, who defied the Governor to do his worst, and in violent language swore that he was prepared to risk everything, finally had to be removed from office.

The anxieties of the Governor were increased when a formal demand was received from the Court for a share in the elephant trade. Evasive replies were given, but the Ministers refused to be put off in this fashion, and time after time repeated their demand ; they ended by insisting further on the opening of the port of Puttalam. The Batavian authorities were applied to for instructions. They hesitated and finessed, but at last plucked up courage to give a decided answer. Early in 1757 Jan Schreuder, a native of Hamburg who had risen from the ranks of the army, arrived as successor to Loten, and the two of them conveyed to the Sinhalese ambassadors then at Colombo, the final decision refusing to concede either request.

CHAPTER VI.

"The pitcher which had gone so often to water became leaky by degrees and broke to pieces in my hand at a wrathful push of the displeased Court" wrote Schreuder as he left the country in March 1762. The shrewd van Imhoff had foretold the probable result of the Company's policy, and it was the misfortune of Schreuder that the catastrophe took place during his administration. A hundred years had passed since the expulsion of the Portuguese, and before narrating the incidents which led up to the approaching crisis, it is convenient to pause a moment and to inquire whether the Netherlands Company had justified its existence.

The Hollander declared, as unctuously as is usual, that God had entrusted him with a special mission to conquer, and incidentally to exploit, the heathen, and it might well be that some Hollanders really did believe in this profession. The exploiting of the country was the main object of the Company; this object rendered it necessary that there should be peace, and that the people should have the opportunity of developing on certain lines the latent resources at their disposal; and the result was a degree of peace and well-being which formed a satisfactory contrast to the state of things which prevailed under the Portuguese. No oppression or violence of an exceptional nature was permitted save what was dictated by the requirements of a Company of Merchants who desired heavy dividends.

Naturally enough the Company preferred to have Europeans in all lucrative posts, and nearly every race of Europe was represented in its service and were known to the natives by the common name of Hollanders. Only people born in Europe were officially classed as European. The children of a European father born in the country were called *pusties*, and the children of *pusties*, named *casties*, were classed as natives. It was recognised that such natives were less competent than Europeans, and as no question of returning home could arise with them, they were paid at a lower rate than Europeans. The Mestici were the offspring of mixed marriages with the Asiatic races. The men of all these classes, as well as the Tupasses and the descendants of freed slaves, dressed alike; while among the women the Mestici, Tupasses and freed slaves had a costume of their own, which differed from that worn by the rest.

As there was no recognised body on the spot authorised to check the actions of the Executive, it is hardly necessary to say that acts of nepotism were notoriously common. For instance a scullion from Europe who had been house-steward to the Governor, was placed in charge of the fort of Negombo, while an ex-tailor was appointed to a similar position at Trincomalee. The son-in-law, actual or prospective, of an influential official, was sure of preferment, and excuses were easily found for new appointments. The public service was overstaffed, and the allowances of cash, rice and other rations granted to all the Company's servants were a heavy drain on its resources. The system of perquisites, a legacy from the Portuguese, had a depressing effect on trade; everyone selling to the Company was expected to allow an overcharge, which in the case of pepper amounted to 12½ per cent, and this excess was divided among certain favoured officials.

There was much dishonesty prevalent, and van Gollenesse had to order the prosecution of several prominent public servants. "Who loves the truth" wrote Schreuder when referring to them, "cannot deny that the greater part had been awaked by me as it were from the sleep of laziness and carelessness, and I kept them awake by continual inciting, earnest admonitions, threats and fines." Indeed it is known that one Commandeur at Jafanapatnam saved himself the trouble of thinking, by passing over to his Secretary a blank sheet signed by himself at the bottom, to be filled in with such orders as the Secretary thought fit.

The Company in Ceylon strangely failed to live up to the reputation of the United Provinces for legal instinct. It was still possible for the Governor in 1751 to complain that the officers of the Chief Court had no knowledge of law, and that as a consequence their decisions were frequently upset on Appeal at Batavia. Intermeddlers and unlicensed Proctors exercised as evil an influence in the Courts as they do now.

"If there is any point of administration as regards the natives of Ceylon that may be called intricate and almost infeasible, it is that concerning the possession and mortgaging of land.* " This opinion was expressed by van Imhoff in 1740, and no Government has yet faced the situation with courage. He found that the Landraad had ceased to exist save at Matara, and the hardworked Merchant who held the office of Disawa was expected to deal with this extremely complicated subject in addition to his numerous other trade and administrative duties. The result was that land disputes were usually referred to native Commissioners, and, just as it had been under the Portuguese, it was soon found out that the Disawa's Interpreter or Attapattu Mudaliyar, was the real umpire in these cases.

---

* Van Imhoff's Memoir, p. 20.

Those abuses which always must be expected as long as public officers are incompetent to carry on public business in the language used by the public, prevailed in all directions. In addition there was that delay of justice which is not less hurtful than injustice, and lands which were the subject of dispute lay uncultivated for many years pending a decision. Van Imhoff therefore urged the re-establishment of the Landraad both at Galle and Colombo, and his recommendation was accepted. Two new Courts were opened, and sat for two days in the week to dispose of land suits, monthly reports being sent to the Governor of the work done. These Courts were strictly enjoined to bring to the notice of Government any case in which the instructions laid down for their guidance were opposed to the custom of the country.

The Jaffna Tombo had been kept up and renewed every fifteen years, the last revision being in 1754; a Head Tombo was prepared for the Manar District; but in the South the condition of things was not satisfactory. It was an early discovery that one of the surest ways to secure the peace of a harassed official was to refuse the public access to public registers; accordingly de Heere "of blessed memory" had ordered the Portuguese Tombo of Colombo, over which Antao Vaz Freire had toiled for so many years a century before, to be burnt. No systematic effort had been made since to prepare a new Tombo, though various local Rolls dealing with minor matters such as Arecanut and Cinnamon were in existence, till in 1739 the work was started in the Matara Disawani.

The Tombo now prepared was a register showing all persons and landed property in the country, arranged according to provinces and districts. An examination of this shewed at a glance the complete extent of the occupied territory, the number of the population, the services the inhabitants were liable to perform to the Company, the duty they had to pay for their lands, the denominations under which the lands were assessed, the title of parties thereto, what *badawedili* and other privileges they enjoyed, and what unoccupied lands were available for disposal.

In the case of lands belonging to the Company which had been planted with its consent, a third of the produce was claimed for the Company, and a half where there had been no consent. Where no documentary title could be proved, they were treated as Company's land planted without consent. There were various classes of *Paraveni* land, which formed the nearest approach to tenure in fee simple; where there were documents to show that all the Company's claims had been paid, or that the lands had been given free of all dues in reward for services rendered, no duty was levied. The largest group of this class consisted of the Service Paraveni lands which were held subject to *Rajakariya* or service to Government in accordance with caste and birth. Such lands descended to a man's heirs with the same liability attached thereto and could not be mortgaged or sold. Where the tenant received promotion to a higher grade as by appointment to a Mudaliyarship, the services in connection with these lands had to be performed by a substitute, or a duty paid. *Malapala* lands were those which had lapsed to Government on failure of heirs, and *Nilapala* those which were abandoned either because of their lack of fertility, an out-break of small-pox, or some similar reason. All such were again at the disposal of the Company, which re-allotted them, usually as *Badawedili.*

As for the rice fields, those from which the Company derived a profit consisted of the ancient royal *Muttettu,* which the inhabitants had to cultivate for its benefit free of charge, and the *Ande* and *Otu* fields on which the cultivators paid a half and a tenth of the crop respectively as the Company's share. Both van Gollenesse and Schreuder urged the advantages to be gained by transplanting the paddy plant, but without the slightest effect.

The preparation of the Tombo was a matter of much labour and delay; opposition, mostly passive, was encountered on every side: the Council was kept busy with resolutions for compelling registration, and the free transfer of property was greatly hampered. The Colombo Tombo which was begun in 1742 was completed by August 1759, when an immediate revision was ordered. Three years later the Galle Tombo was nearly complete; while that of Matara, which was begun first of all and which caused most trouble, came to an untimely end, as will be seen later.

The efficient administration of the country depended on the efficiency of the native chiefs and headmen, through whom all administrative acts had to be carried out. Over every Korale there was a Mudaliyar who was in charge of the Lascarins of the Korale, as well as a Korale Vidane, now called Korala, who looked after the revenue interests of the Company, supervised the cultivation of lands, and collected dues. The Korala was assisted by Atu Koralas, and Vidanes were appointed over groups of villages.

There had set in a tendency to increase to an unreasonable extent the number of these officials, and all of them had to be provided for. The chief defect in the system of appointments arose from the acknowledged fact that bribery was largely instrumental in securing posts, the consequence being that it was not always that the best men were selected, while naturally the successful candidates expected to recoup themselves for their expenditure by fleecing the villagers. The unhealthy craving for petty titles and distinctions, entailing as it must always do the destruction of independence and self-respect, was as strong then as it is now, and everyone who was connected with parties in office expected to be remembered.

Van Imhoff advised the reduction in the number of these offices; where possible he combined the office of Korala with that of Mudaliyar, and he also suggested that in the more important divisions the Atukoralas should be raised to the rank of Mohundirams. He was anxious that complaints against them should not be suppressed but carefully inquired into, for he realised how often there was reason for the complaint, and how difficult if not impossible it was for the villager to prove his case against anyone in power.

The remuneration given to these officers was considered excessive. There was no fixed rule on the subject, and the amount was left to the humour of the Governor. A Mudaliyar who received an extensive *Badawedilla* did not trouble to have the less fertile land cultivated, or to put what he had to the best use possible. It was not unusual to allot an entire village to an individual, as had been the custom under the Sinhalese Kings, and in such a case the grantee became entitled to receive all the revenue which the Company used to obtain therefrom, subject to the payment of a small quit-rent.

Nearly the whole of the Pasdun and Galle Korales had thus been given away, and encroachments made even on Gampaha and Weke, the two ancient *Gabadagam* which were of such value for provisioning the garrisons of Negumbo and Hanwella. The village Mayorals, the real husbandmen, who had heavy duties to perform, were neglected, with the result that their number steadily diminished, as people preferred to be ranked as Lascarins, when they received comfortable *badawedili* and were liable to little service.

Van Gollenesse followed the principles indicated by Van Imhoff and cut down the number of offices with a ruthless hand. He also framed a scheme for the allotment of *Badawedili* lands, laying down how much each public servant was to receive, from the 20 *amunams* of the Maha Mudaliyar, to the 20 *bera* of the village tom-tom beater or *Gam berawaya.* Moreover he took action to get back for the Company or to levy a duty on all lands which had been given away without sufficient reason or at an undervaluation. It was at the same time enacted that in future no *Sannas* conveying land was to be written on palm leaf, but only on paper signed by the Governor himself, an exception being made in the case of *badawedili* given to Lascarins.

The old body of Mudaliyars with their extensive grants had died away by the time he left, and only the aged Anthonan de Saram Mudaliyar, father of the Maha Mudaliyar, and Tilakaratna of Matara, son of the renegade Punchi Appuhami, still remained; the consequence was that a large amount of valuable land had reverted to the Company. Orders were also given to reduce the number of Lascarins, whose services now consisted mainly in carrying messages and capturing runaway slaves; in 1745 the number of *ranchu* for the Colombo Disavani was fixed at one hundred and five. Artisans such as carpenters and sawyers who received pay for their services, were not provided with *badawedili.*

Schreuder was not able to report much improvement in the difficult question of the native officers, but he was prepared to see that charges were often made against them without foundation by parties interested in creating vacancies. He was at one time inclined to recommend that these offices should be made hereditary in the families of the more deserving, but as he realised that this would exclude a large number whose claims were entitled to consideration, he desisted from doing so.

Besides the payments of rice already referred to, there were numerous other sources of revenue which though not of much pecuniary importance, were nevertheless of interest. There were first of all the Alphandigo or Customs; the *Pol-aya,* consisting of a tenth of the yield from all coconut trees; and the *decum* which was in the nature of a poll tax. The toddy and arrack rents never yielded very much. Then there were the Bazaar rents, and the dues from the fisheries, fishing boats, and nets. The Company had various gardens, including a tobacco plantation at Negombo and a coconut land of fifteen thousand trees at Galkissa, which were leased out, as well as certain gemming rights in the Matara District and in the Colombo Disavani.

The gem country was mainly within the King's Dominions, and was kept jealously guarded; no mining was permitted without his special order and everything found was reserved for his use; all trade in gems was discouraged, though occasionally fakirs would smuggle valuable specimens across the border. Gem cutting was carried on by the Moors of Matara. In Jaffna there were moreover the stamping of cloth, and brokerage fees on tobacco and jaggery. At Manar the feeding of cattle under the tank beds was a source of profit, and certain dues were paid in *ghi* or butter. The right to winnow the sand at the site of the Fishery was also sold. Perhaps as interesting as any was the tax levied on the humble Moor and Chetty who desired to wear the loose slippers called *Papus,* sandals, or any other footgear.

Originally the majority of the dues were collected on behalf of the Company, but it was found more profitable to farm out the right to recover them, and at Colombo this was done every August by public auction.

Since 1732 there had been no pearl fishery. It should be realised that the profits which the Company derived from a fishery did not arise directly from the oysters, but indirectly from levies on the boats engaged; fees, varying according to religion, payable by the divers; import duties, etc. Indeed as a rule the Company found it very difficult to secure any pearls even by purchase, in consequence of the keen competition of the Indian merchants. Against these profits had to be set off the heavy expense of organising the fishery and maintaing guards, the chances of an outbreak of illness amongst the great assembly, and the certainty of much smuggling and the dislocation of the usual trade of the Company.

In view of all this van Imhoff recommended that the right of fishery should be sold by public auction, and this advice being adopted, the right to fish for thirty days with 600 men was sold, and for the five years following 1746 the Company obtained a large profit without incurring any risk whatever. This created much interest at Court, and in 1750 twenty-one of the King's vessels appeared off Chilaw and dived for oysters. The Company's vessels hovered about, for the Hollanders were not prepared to admit the right of the King to any *dominium maris* or to any oysters; fortunately none were found, and thus complications were avoided. There was no fishery during the time of Schreuder.

Among other sources of revenue from the sea were the chanks which were imported to India; the cowries from the Maldives, which were in great demand in Europe for the African slave trade; and shark skins which were exported for covering the sword-handles of Japanese Daimios. It was however recognised that the wealth of Ceylon lay in its agricultural products. The increasing demand for coffee, which had been introduced among Europeans in the middle of the seventeenth century and was fast revolutionising their social manners, drew the attention of the Company to the possibility of its growth in the Island, and in September, 1720, Rumpf issued a proclamation worded with all the skill of a modern advertising agent, urging the people to take up its cultivation. The advantages of the new product were soon realised, and the terms offered by the Company were more liberal than were usual in its dealings: for the main difficulty experienced in persuading the natives to take up any new cultivation was their not groundless fear that it would entail some new duty to Government.

Cultivation was rapidly taken in hand, and once again the energetic Wijayawardhana received from the Company on a plate of gold an acknowledgment of the zeal displayed by him. The Mudaliyar died shortly after, having served the Company for forty six years.

A special officer was appointed to supervise the cultivation, but he soon proved a source of oppression to the people, who had to supply provisions for him and his attendants during his frequent tours. The native officials therefore unanimously requested Pielat to abolish the office, promising an increased quantity of coffee if they were relieved of his exactions; the office was abolished and the supply from Colombo was immediately doubled, till in 1739 a hundred thousand pounds were exported. The output from Java and the West Indies had in the meantime attained such dimensions that the price fell heavily and the Company began to discourage the cultivation. The result was that the plantations were soon neglected, and the berries lay uncollected on the ground, for the people had not yet learnt to drink coffee. Then came a ruinous war in Java which lasted from 1741 to 1758, and the supply was so reduced that orders were received by Schreuder to buy up all the coffee available, and the prospects of the enterprise were again bright.

Cardamoms were obtained almost exclusively from the King's country, by way of Matara, and the troubles with the Court so affected the supply that the article nearly disappeared from the trade returns; Versluys therefore attempted to persuade the people in the Galle and Matara Districts to grow the finer but smaller Malabar variety, though with little success. The Company then increased the price it was prepared to pay and thus succeeded in keeping up a fairly satisfactory supply. Van Imhoff however discovered some of the Malabar plants growing at Hanwella in the garden of Paulo Alvis Mudaliyar, the able and energetic Chief of the Hewagam Korale, and the latter was instructed to open up a plantation. This was done and van Gollenesse was able to report a large increase, though white ants sadly damaged the garden at Eswatta. The cultivation spread into the Siyane and Pasdun Korales, but the trouble caused by the white ants was so great that in 1757 instructions were received from Batavia to discontinue the attempt.

Pepper again was an article which first the Portuguese and after them the Hollanders had made several attempts to develop, for there were heavy profits to be made from it, and a large quantity was required every year for packing with the cinnamon which was shipped. Versluys had taken much interest in the matter, and van Imhoff tried to persuade the Court as well to take up the subject. Many Sinhalese availed themselves of the eagerness of the Company to obtain for themselves large tracts of good land under agreement to plant the vine, and these lands were then utilised for other purposes.

In spite of much opposition the cultivation gradually spread; Don Bastian, the Mitrigala Vidane, opened two plantations which were described as the two most beautiful gardens in the Siyane Korale, though the Korala who was jealous of his success attempted to undo his work by removing the coolies who had been placed at his disposal. The excessive drought of 1750 badly damaged most of the plantations. An attempt was made to force the people by *plakaats* to take up the cultivation, but Schreuder pointed out that he did much more to increase the supply by raising the price moderately and treating the producer well than his predecessors had done by their appeal to compulsion. In 1753 the export nearly reached the figure of 300,000 lbs.

Arecanut continued to yield abundant profits, and in 1746 more than 18000 amunams were exported; but the system under which it was collected and the small price offered by the Company to the owners killed all desire to increase the supply; on the other hand very often everything beyond the amount required to meet the Company's duty was left to rot under the trees as not worth the trouble of collecting. The Company therefore had recourse to some of the Moormen of Galle and Matara and entrusted the collection to them under promise of handsome payment for any quantity delivered beyond the Company's duty.

The profits were somewhat affected by the competition of the English areca from Atchin, but much more by the smuggling which was still carried on boldly. The remedy which was suggested by some was to abolish the monopoly and throw open the trade to everyone, subject to a duty for purposes of revenue; but such a scheme was too much in advance of the times to be favourably considered.

The cultivation of coconut was rapidly increasing, not only along the sea coast to the South of Colombo, and in the Peninsula of Kalpitiya, but inland as well. The planting with coconut of forest which might contain cinnamon was not regarded with much favour, for the revenue derivable from coconuts was small. Indeed Schreuder complained bitterly "where one saw formerly twenty or thirty peelers' tents pitched, one now finds nothing but coconut gardens." The owners distilled arrack from the produce of their trees, after paying a small fee to the toddy renter, and the shipping and the garrisons were supplied with this spirit, which it was believed "used moderately does as much good to our people as it does harm when taken in large quantities".* The main centre of distillation was along the coast from Colombo to Matara, and extending three miles inland; north of Colombo "pot-stills" were in use as in the time of the Sinhalese Kings. The privilege of the arrack renter to demoralise a non-drinking population was confined to the limited rented area round towns and military stations; and the introduction of the liquor within the interior was forbidden and the headmen were expected to see to the prohibition being enforced. As a rule taverns had to be closed at 8 p. m; they were recognised as centres where gamblers and vagrants collected, and where stolen property could conveniently be disposed of.

There were however aspects of the Company's activities other than the mercantile which have to be considered. As early as 1685 the Chief Physician had drawn the attention of the authorities to the alarming prevalence of a disease, described as leprosy, among the children of the Hollanders by their native or Mestico wives. Steps were taken to segregate the affected persons and in the time of Simons a spacious Asylum was erected at Hendala, which is in use down to the present day.

The zeal which at one time marked the Company's attempts to educate the people and to convert them into the "true Reformed Faith" had exhausted itself, and the villager's experience of the blessings which the religion of the foreigner was expected to bring, had not been such as to destroy his inherited love for the hoary religion of his ancestors. The formulae which the Portuguese priest had taught as the one true religion today might well excite a smile. But that priest was inspired by a passionate, though perhaps not always a scrupulous, devotion, which still carried him

* *Zwardecroon's Memoir p. 73.*

within the territory which the Company now administered. Repressive measures followed, and in 1699 on the orders of van Rheede, all Roman Catholic Churches and secret conventicles were closed; but it was a shock to the officers of the Company when they discovered eight years later that the bulk of the thirty five churches in Jaffna were well stocked with heathen literature.

It was impossible to blink the fact that the natives were at heart heathen. The Wannias for instance had all been baptised, but they were more than suspected of being "devil-worshippers" which probably meant Hindus, and their resolute refusal to admit Europeans within their houses aggravated the suspicion. Becker tried the effect of legislation, and in a proclamation of the 6th of June, 1711, declared that whereas, "The clear instructions which we have constantly issued to dispel the darkness that surrounds the people of this country are to our immeasureable sorrow and great displeasure daily disobeyed and insulted, we find it expedient to awaken that attention which our blessed religion requires". This was to be effected by enacting that anyone found at a place of heathen worship or decorating heathen images or taking part in Hindu ceremonies was liable to be summarily arrested and punished corporally as well as by rigorous imprisonment. At the same time all priests officiating at the *Dewalayas* were ordered to leave the Company's territory.

No one paid much attention to the proclamation, which was supported by a subsequent order forbidding Christians to marry Buddhists. This too was found to be not sufficiently effective, and in 1760 it was considered necessary to disgrace the Statute Book by an Ordinance to the effect that if a Christian woman lived with a pagan man, the two of them were liable to be flogged till blood appeared, to be branded, confined in chains at hard labour for life to have all their property confiscated, and their children taken for slaves. Yet in the Nanayakkara School at Matara, which was reserved for the high-class Appuhamis, none of the desired children were to be found, as they had Buddhist priests at home to instruct them.

The public chastisement of headmen for allowing heathen practises had little effect so long as the higher clergy showed little energy. The Hollander lacked the zeal of the Portuguese, and it is not possible to speak of him as a missionary. The clergyman was little more than a State official; his annual visit was as much of a nuisance and source of expense to the villager as that of a revenue officer. Villages with a reputation for fat chickens and good mutton, which the inhabitants had to supply free of cost, never lacked the ministrations of these clergy, who frequently took their wives with them, and the public had to supply the necessary palanquin bearers; at the same time they often went to the extent of refusing to visit the more remote and less attractive centres of population, till specific orders were sent for the purpose. Moreover, clergymen were forbidden to baptise slaves, as no Christian could be a slave; the consequence was that to most households there was attached a group of dissolute men and women who exercised a profoundly evil influence on the children.

Christoph Langhansz, a native of Breslau who was in Ceylon in 1696, expressed the opinion that as the Portuguese lost the Island in consequence of their excessive pride, so the Hollanders might some day share the same fate as the result of their excessive avarice and of their neglect to teach Christianity to the heathen. It seemed that they excused themselves for their negligence in this respect by suggesting that "the Providence of the great God could not have wished it otherwise." Some attempt was made to remedy this discouraging state of things. A fine Church was erected within the Fort of Jafanapatnam, where the Church of Our Lady of Miracles had been pulled down in 1692, and another ordered in 1723 at the ancient capital of Kotte. Seminaries were opened both at Jaffna and Colombo for training youths of good family for the Ministry; the first of these was closed before the lapse of many years, while the second continued to exist as one of the institutions favoured by successive Governors.

The students trained within its walls were very few in number and were carefully selected; the Governor and Council were usually present at their examination—indeed in one year the responsible clergy refused to hold the examination because the Governor's carriage had not been sent to convey them. Van Imhoff has recorded his delight at seeing the dusky youths who knew little or no Dutch, talking in Latin or poring over Greek. Annual reports were sent to The XVII in Europe, and selected students completed their course at the Universities of Holland, though The XVII had in 1700 disallowed the proposal, because a similar scheme had proved a failure in Batavia. Wijaya Sriwardana Maha Mudaliyar at one time taught within the walls of the Colombo Seminary; and Henricus Philipsz, the son of van Gollenesse's trusted Maha Mudaliyar Panditaratna, went from it to Utrecht and Amsterdam, and returned as a Predikant to labour among his own people.

Nevertheless Christianity made but small progress; the causes which operate so adversely today acted with equal force under the Company, and Pielat, van Imhoff, and van Gollenesse all complained bitterly that clergymen could not be found who could preach to the people in their own language. The people could not think of a God who had to be addressed in a foreign tongue, and it was here that the far-seeing Church of Rome, which was quick to establish a native ministry wherever it went, found its strength.

In spite of all its efforts the Company could not check the ingratiating influence of that Church. It tried to extirpate Popery by punishing its adherents, forbidding baptism by priests, and rendering the reception of a priest a penal offence. As in the case of Mohammedans and the heathen, their marriages were not considered legal if they did not conform to the regulations of the Company. But the persistence of the Mestico priests from Goa could not be stopped, and they had a large following along the coast from Jaffna to Matara.

It is true that the religion of the converts was described as sitting lightly on them. Jacob Haafner of Halle, a German of wide experience in the Company's Eastern settlements, who was in Ceylon in 1782, has stated that they knew little of Christianity save to make the sign of the cross and to mutter a prayer, the very criticism which had been passed more than a hunderd years before. Elias Paravacini de Capelle of Breda, who had spent more than thirty years in various parts of Ceylon, expressed a similar opinion regarding the Mukkuwas of Puttalam. As a rule, little had been done beyond introducing new incantations and new ceremonies in place of the old.

None the less there were congregations which were prepared to take up a bold attitude on the question of freedom of conscience. For instance in 1750 the Roman Catholics of Negombo presented a memorial written in Tamil, in which while declaring their firm adherence to the religion their ancestors had adopted two hundred years before, they protested against their children being compelled to learn at the schools tenets to which they objected, and they further complained that they were forced by heavy fines to send their children to such schools.

The Consistory to whom the memorial was referred, recommended the strict enforcement of the existing regulations against Popery, and that Romish baptisms and marriages should not be acknowledged, while it further urged that none but Protestants should be appointed as headmen.

The Council, which did not always work in harmony with the Consistory, pointed out in reply that it was not within the province of the latter to offer advice regarding matters of administration; it said that it would greatly regret if it were compelled in making appointments to confine itself to Protestants, and in turn it advised the clergy to learn the native languages sufficiently well to be able to influence the people against Popery.

The Roman Catholics thereupon grew more aggressive; in Puttalam and Kalpitiya one priest obtained a great reputation by exorcising the locusts and beetles which damaged the coconut trees; at Kalutara there were public exhibitions and processsions, till their leader was arrested and banished. At Negombo they insulted the clergy and resorted to open violence. In 1757 on the report of the Scholarchal Commission, the Council ordered some Chapels which had been built there to be pulled down, when the people who were sent to do the work were opposed by a crowd of women. The Disawa therefore sent some Lascarins to enforce compliance; near Toppu they were attacked by a large body of fishermen and the military had to be called out. Some of the ring-leaders were arrested, but Toppu and Pallansena were found deserted, and the inhabitants collected on an Island on the borders of the Company's territory; they would not be persuaded to return, and the military thereupon pulled down the offending structures and withdrew.

In the same year a youth who had been sent from the Seminary to Leyden published in Holland a pamphlet which created a great scandal. He said the ministers worked not for the love of God but merely for gain ; he charged them with apathy ; he declared it was their indolence alone which prevented them from learning the native languages; and asserted that but for the exertions of van Imhoff, the Church in Ceylon would have been as good as dead. This violent attack upon them occasioned much animated discussion among the clergy, who bitterly reproached the outspoken youth for his ingratitude in casting such aspersions on those under whom he had learnt. Some years later the writer returned as an ordained clergymen, when he retracted his observations and brotherly feeling was restored.

Apart from the indifference of the clergy the scandalous lives led by some of the Europeans, including men in high places, proved as much of a stumbling block in the way of conversion, as it had done in the time of the Portuguese. The private life of Van Domburg, when Governor designate, was of so dubious a nature, that serious reports had to be sent to Batavia on the subject. Not unnaturally the natives were unable to understand why that which was a penal offence when committed by them, passed unnoticed when done by a Hollander. So lax was the European congregation at Colombo, which numbered a thousand souls, that barely fifty could be found to attend the Church service on Sunday. The completion in 1749 of a noble church at Wolvendahl did little to remedy matters.

The Scholarchal Commission was in charge of the education of the country. This Board had the supervision of all native Christians, dealt with their matrimonial matters, and saw to the proper preparation of the School Tombos. These were registers containing a record of the domestic history of each individual; they showed who and what his parents and family were ; when he was born, baptized and married, what education he had, when he died and what family he left behind. The Board appointed two inspectors who visited the schools once a year to report on the progress made, to check the registers, and to audit the fines which were freely imposed to persuade villagers to attend school and church. They moreover baptised the children and performed the marriage service of Christians whose Banns had been duly published in the course of the previous year. Such publication even came to be regarded as itself an informal rite which entitled the parties to live as husband and wife pending the performance of the yearly religious service.

It was not always that the Board displayed energy, and for the five years prior to 1703 it never met at all. The schools throughout the Island were neglected, the buildings in many cases fell into decay, and the very beams were stolen from them. After a period of fitful energy the troubles of 1735 nearly destroyed all school operations. Van Imhoff however took an active interest in the subject, and the establishment of a printing press in 1736 was considered likely to mark the commencement of a great change for the better. Various edifying books and tracts were issued from it, but there was little practical improvement.

In 1760 the basis of education at the Colombo Seminary was widened so as to enable suitable youths to be trained there to be chief headmen and schoolmasters, and careful regulations were drawn up anew for the purpose. At the same time their preparation for the ministry was discouraged.

No provision appears to have been made for the education of girls, but what was even more remarkable was the negligence of the Company in regard to the sons of its European servants. Eschelskroon, a German with much experience of the East, published in 1784 a short account of Ceylon, in which he drew attention to this omission. The East was an unhealthy atmosphere for European children;

few parents were in a position to send them to Europe for their education, while the very large majority allowed them to grow up in their homes as best they could. Their chief companions were the numerous slaves who surrounded them, and it was mainly from these slaves that the rising generation of Hollanders imbibed their views of life.

Flattery and adulation were their daily food, and they gradually learnt to consider themselves so superior to those around them, that they needed not to acquire even a little book learning or adequately qualify themselves for future service. In the few cases where a proper tutor was provided, the influence of the familiar slaves soon destroyed the effect of such moral teaching as he conveyed to them. The result was that the Ceylon-born Hollander degenerated rapidly, and his ambition did not extend much beyond eating and drinking. Such masters as were to be found in the schools were, if Eschelskroon is to be trusted, the so-called "chaplains that come with the ships from Europe, or more usually still, broken mechanics, such as bakers, shoe-makers, glaziers, etc."

CHAPTER VII.

Kirti Sri Raja Sinha had married in addition to his first Queen two others, the daughters of Gabbedature Nayaker and Rama Nayaker, and the relatives of the new Queens had accompanied them to Court till it assumed a "novel, namely a Malabar, countenance", as Schreuder remarked. It is true that Sinhalese noblemen still continued to be the King's Ministers, but the real force behind the Throne consisted of his Malabar kinsmen. Chief among them was his own father, Narenappa Nayaker, a determined and resourceful man, and a strict disciplinarian. The Sinhalese officials were watched with the utmost jealousy by the King, who feared any combination among them; they were supervised by the Malabars who filled the most lucrative appointments and for whose maintenance a large revenue was required.

Mampitiya, now advanced in years and blind, wielded great influence at Court, and his ripe experience and sound judgment always commanded respect. The King, who had no children by his Queens, had taken as his *Yakada Doliya* the daughter of Mampitiya's son, the late Bintenne Disawa. She had borne him a son and two daughters, and the King's passionate attachment to her greatly strengthened the position of Mampitiya.

Schreuder had made repeated attempts to purchase the goodwill of the leading Ministers, but he was obliged at last ruefully to confess that with one exception their moral rectitude had been proot against his blandishments. The exception was in the case of

Dumbara, who was still in charge of the Three and Four Korales. All communications with the Ministers except the annual letter to Court, were carried on either by the Disawa of Colombo or by the Maha Mudaliyar, through this Disawa of the King, and in consequence his goodwill was worth a great deal to the Company. Dumbara Rala therefore received from it an annual allowance of six thousand rix dollars, and in addition valuable presents were sent to him from time to time.

It is a question whether Dumbara merely was trading upon the gullibility of the Company or not, for when matters reached a crisis he showed himself an able and trustworthy servant of the King; but for the present he was hinting that the allowance might be increased with advantage to both sides.

The one thought which engrossed the attention of the Company's officers who desired to win the approbation of the Directors in Europe, was how to secure the ten thousand bales of cinnamon which were required every year, and which formed the main item of the Company's profits. This anxiety created a most humiliating state of things, which Schreuder felt acutely. "In the whole of India," he wrote, "no product is so miserably ill-conditioned. . . . If one knew the difficulties and inconveniences it occasioned, how the Company from time to time humbled itself to the whimsical Court for that small bark, and what we have suffered for it, one would acknowledge that the collection of the cinnamon finally depended on a phantastical Prince and the whimsicalities of his covetous courtiers."

Every year a special embassy had to be sent to secure with abject genuflexions the right to collect it in the King's dominions, and every year the cinnamon had to be fetched like "a firebrand from the fire" with heartburnings and anxiety as to whether it would be in time for the sailing season.

No sooner was one difficulty overcome than another was raised by the ingenuity of the courtiers, till the stuff finally reached the Company's territory. The Chalias served as a convenient tool for worrying the Hollanders; at a hint from Court they would disappear into the King's dominions, where it was not possible to reach them, and without them there could be no peeling. Often they had to be coaxed back with a promise that even the ringleaders would not be punished; but "a Governor would rather venture everything and even sacrifice a part of his own possessions, than fail in sending cinnamon."

Similar tactics were followed in the case of the elephants; each year leave had to be obtained to convey them to Jaffna over the King's territory, but the moment they reached the border difficulties would be raised by the petty officials, and all manner of serious delay created by references to headquarters. Similarly when timber had to be felled near Batticaloa, where it was abundant, it was found that permission to fell was not the same as permission for the woodcutters to enter the kingdom, or permission to remove the timber when felled. As it took four weeks for a letter to reach Colombo from Batticaloa, the seriousness to the Company of these tactics can well be realised.

Desertions by the Company's subjects were so frequent that military men were forbidden to cross the *Kadawatu* without a pass; a reward of ten rix dollars was promised to anyone who arrested such deserters, and half that sum where the deserter was a slave. There was the same trouble with the King over these men, and only now and then would he be persuaded to surrender a few slaves or cinnamon peelers, usually on the condition that they would not be punished; this naturally encouraged desertion.

Often the King would capriciously close his *Kadawatu* and prohibit the export of grain from his country and thus cause much distress among the Company's subjects. The reason for all this was not hard to find. "The Court for the last nine years first requested, then demanded, next insisted, now in a most insolent manner has sought to compel us, to permit it to share in the most substantial and considerable monopolies and branches of the Company's trade, viz., Areca and Elephants", complained Schreuder.

The change was very great from the days when the Company thought that the Court was being "hoodwinked with outward pomp, caresses and compliments." The Nayakers at Court brought with them the larger experience of India, and the Ministers were no longer prepared to allow their country to be a milch—cow for the benefit of the Company, or to permit the latter to control the entire coast.

Schreuder could see the reasonableness of their attitude; he admitted that where it was rendered worth the while of the Sinhalese, no difficulty arose with reference to the supply of goods. He anticipated that if the cinnamon which was taken from the King's dominions were paid for, everybody would be satisfied. He could see even further; in the Company's own territory the name of cinnamon was loathed. It only reminded the people of harsh measures against the destruction of the wild plant, restrictions on the development of valuable lands, incursions by the rough Chalias on private property, and generally discomfort and loss. The very crows which served to distribute the wild seed, might not be killed, in spite of all the damage they caused. Everyone therefore took a delight in destroying the hated plant whenever they could do so with safety, and the supply obtainable within its territory was diminishing at a rate which caused alarm.

Schreuder pointed out that if the cultivation was thrown open to everyone, on condition that they sold the produce to the Company at a reasonable fixed rate, there need no longer be any anxiety about the supply. His views were not acceptable to the Batavian authorities, and were rewarded with a private reprimand.

The next best policy, indeed the only other one open if force was to be avoided, was that of obsequiousness to the King, who called them his "faithful Hollanders, the guardians of his coast." The Sinhalese view of the relation which existed between the King and the Company is thus stated by the writer of the *Mahawansa* .... "The Hollanders, who were powerful merchants, had been appointed in the time of Raja Sinha to defend the Island and continued to perform the duties of messengers to the Kings of Lanka. It was their custom to bring presents of great value every year, with much honour and in great procession."

Schreuder regarded the matter from a different standpoint. "We cannot stir," he grumbled, "much less make proper profit of this conquest, if we do not continually, indeed, nauseatingly, flatter and caress the Court; and though this is commonly called by us, keeping the Court in good humour, it tends to the great degradation of the Honourable Company, which formerly made itself so feared in this country, but now almost continually has to play the lying little poodle."

At the same time, he pointed out, all the time-honoured means adopted to weaken the King were to be followed; all dissensions at Court, all dissatisfaction among his people, were to be encouraged and utilised for the benefit of the Company. It was found however that this was less easy now, when the Disawas were responsible directly to the Court, than in former times when there were feudatory Princes, but slightly controlled by the King, to whom they rendered only certain nominal services.

The King had two brothers, the younger of whom was born in Ceylon, and the relations which existed between them were of the most affectionate kind. They had received the status of sub-kings and were even permitted to use the Royal Parasol, and establishments which were almost regal had been provided for them. They were heartily in sympathy with the Buddhist tendencies of their brother, and themselves took an active part in endowing monasteries and training priests. "These three brothers" says the writer of the Mahawansa, "having obtained and divided among themselves a kingdom, contended not with each other for greatness. They dwelt together in one city and clave to each other like their own shadows. This I say is a marvellous thing."

Moreover the subserviency of the Company created a dangerous condition of things among its own subjects. They were filled with the idea that their real lord was the King, that they served the Company only with his permission, and that on his orders such service must cease. There was an intimate correspondence between them and the Court, which was kept well informed of everything that took place. The danger of such intercourse between members of one race was recognised, but not all the efforts of the Company could check it. Karunaratna himself incurred the suspicion of Schreuder, and in spite of the fact that such a proceeding was likely to offend the Court, he in 1758 was arrested suddenly and banished to the Cape from where he did not return for many years. It was realised that the King could with the greatest ease upset all the plans of the Company, and that if the latter were not prepared "to dance according to the King's pipes," at a nod from him the flame of revolt would run from Korale to Korale.

There had been unrest, especially in the South, from the commencement of Schreuder's tenure of office; this had been checked by treating the chief headmen with sternness, and holding them responsible for any outbreak; Tennekon Mudaliyar, grand-son of the great Disawa, who was Gajanayaka at Matara, was banished at the same time.

However the feeling among the people was growing in bitterness, especially as the result of the harsh measures adopted by Schreuder to reclaim for the Company lands which had long been possessed by the villagers, but for which no documentary title could be produced. The manner in which the most valuable public records had disappeared should have taught the Company's officers that villagers could not be expected to preserve their palm-leaf scrolls for any length of time in huts which were exposed to the inroads of termites. The ferocious de Azavedo himself had admitted one and a half centuries before the reasonableness of the plea of the loss of such documents.

Entire districts within the Company's territory had been abandoned on the orders of Raja Sinha, and the inhabitants withdrawn among the mountains; these men were now coming back to find their lands under forest or in the occupation of others. This was the cause of much litigation before the Landraad, and of much opposition to the Tombo. Owing to the abject poverty of the villagers they could not be forced to purchase back that share of their lands which the Company claimed, and accordingly men accompanied by a military force, were sent into the country to cut down the coconut trees which they had grown.

Matters were so bad that in some parts of the Colombo Disawani the villagers threatened to abandon their homes and go away, rather than submit to the new exactions. There was also much discontent regarding the manner in which the dues from the rice fields were collected by the renters. At last in 1760 the exasperated inhabitants rose in a general rebellion which, spreading with rapidity throughout the Sinhalese provinces, was so determined in its character that the Company was at its wits, end.

For several months the country was in the hands of a riotous mob which burnt down the schools and rest-houses and destroyed even the Landraad House at Galle. To aggravate the situation the Chalias, prodably acting on a hint from the Court, set fire to the cinnamon they had collected and fled within the King's dominions. The Sinhalese appealed to the King for redress of their grievances, and he expostulated with the Company. At the end of the year affairs were in a less anxious condition.

Fortunately for the Company the King was busy with his own troubles. Whether as the result of the machinations from Colombo, or of the dislike of the courtiers to a Dravidian King, a conspiracy had been formed to kill Kirti Sri, and to place on the throne a youth said to be of the royal family, who had been ordained as a priest in Siam. The conspirators invited the King to hear the preaching of *Bana* at the Poya Maluwa, and on the way they hoped to entice him into a pitfall. Everything was ready, the pitfall was prepared with deadly spikes of *kitul* and arecawood, and concealed under the spathes of the plantain tree covered over with cloth, when the King received information of what was on foot.

The informant was Gopala Mudiyanse, a member of a Mohammedan family of doctors residing in the Four Korales, which had been prominent in the time even of the Portuguese, who seems to have conveyed the news to Galegoda Rala. An inquiry was held and the conspirators arrested. Samanakoddy the Second Adigar, and three of the ring-leaders, were executed at Ampitiya. The Sangha Raja, and Tibbatuwawa, the Maha Nayaka of Malwatta, were suspected of complicity; the former was placed in custody at Kehelella and the latter deprived of his office and imprisoned in the Bintenna. Gopala was rewarded with the lands of Moladanda Rala, one of the conspirators, and Pilima Talauwa was appointed Second Adigar, as Galegoda had succeeded Ehelepola on the Latter's death which occured about this time. The energy and decision with which Narenappa Nayaker acted during the crisis greatly added to the strength of his position at Court.

The King now openly took the part of the rebels and early in 1761 armed men poured across the frontiers. Schreuder was distracted. The one thing which the Company was anxious to avoid was war, and indeed it was hopelessly unprepared for fighting. Its various garrisons consisted of men who had been sent out from Europe under the name of soldiers, but very few of whom had ever handled a musket before, much less had any knowledge of practical warfare. They idled away their time with their Sinhalese partners, who exercised so strong a hold over them that the women were credited with using love potions. Though a soldier could rise to the position of a Staff Officer, yet, as Schreuder complained, "the name of soldier seems to many to be low and common." The artillery was in charge of eighty men, of whom the Constables knew nothing beyond a few figures from their instruction books, while their assistants were only fit to apply the match; there was not one who knew how to set a mortar or train a gun. In the whole country there was not a capable engineer, while the surveyors were so ignorant that the country was still unmapped and the various routes little known.

The officials at Colombo hesitated, but the Sinhalese did not leave them much time for deliberation. Palingupana Rala, with the men of Uva, hurried down to the south. Don Constantyn Ekanayaka, whose father and grandfather had been Mudaliyars and Adigars of Matara, and who in addition had the great influence of the Wijayawardhana and Tennekon families behind him, deserted to the King. The fort of Matara was stormed, its garrison put to the sword, and the artillery carried away in triumph. Everything which was there, including the new Tombo which had been prepared with so much trouble, as well as the Portuguese Tombo of Matara, was destroyed.

The Sinhalese then went and encamped at some distance from the town; here they were surprised by a force which had been sent by sea, whereupon they abandoned the captured guns and withdrew. Another body of men attacked Kalutara. Dumbara Rala himself led an army against Hanwella which in turn was stormed, and the entire garrison put to the sword with the exception of two officers who were taken away as prisoners. All the outlying districts, which were seething with discontent, were occupied on behalf of the King, and Colombo was as good as blockaded.

The two Sinhalese Generals returned to their country and after prostrating themselves at the feet of the King, reported to him what each had achieved. Each was rewarded with a tusked elephant, a gold-mounted sword, a collar of gold, and extensive tracts of land.

In the meantime urgent appeals for help had been sent to India and reinforcements were being hurried across from Choromandel and Malabar. The insult to the Company had to be avenged, and it was decided to attack the King within his own frontiers.

The Sinhalese had ceased to be a fighting race; trained soldiers were few, though about a thousand men armed in the European fashion were available near the Court; they had no cannon and not many *Kodituwakku*. However they had not forgotten what the Portuguese wars had taught them, that the finest strategy was to inflict the maximum of loss on the enemy with the minimum of loss to themselves. They knew every inch of their forest-covered country; every path was familiar to them; every crevice in the rocks where a man could shelter himself was prepared for defence. Their natural instinct for guerilla fighting again asserted itself.

The invading army, encumbered with baggage, ill provided with guides, with little experience of warfare, and badly officered, reached the outskirts of the mountains and commenced axe in hand to clear the roads, for none were available save the steepest footpaths. Concealed behind trees the Sinhalese sharpshooters, who were supplied with guns of their own make, and their archers, began to worry the men with little danger to themselves. The drummers were the first victims, for it was they who both inspirited the native levies and also conveyed orders over great distances; it was said that after two days in the forest not a drummer was left. Next came the officers who were conspicuous by their uniforms, which they were soon obliged to change for the dress of privates.

Nightfall, which was expected to bring some relief, only made their situation worse, for the camp-fires threw the harassed troops into greater prominence, while deepening the gloom of the forest were the Sinhalese were concealed. Great trees which had been left half cut through came crashing down on them at the most unexpected places. Boulders thundered down whenever they entered any of the numerous defiles. The baggage and stores of ammunition were soon cut off. One half of the invading army, it was asserted, was destroyed, and the demoralised survivors precipitately retreated, defeated by an enemy whom they had never seen.

The Batavian authorities were in dismay. For a hundred years they successfully had avoided war; they were willing to pay almost any price to secure peace, and they sent their instructions accordingly. The King too did not like the continuance of hostilities and hints were given that an armistice would be not unwelcome.

Petrus Albertus van der Parra had only recently assumed duties as Governor General of Netherlands India, and on the 8th of December 1761 a letter addressed by him to the King reached Colombo in the Company's ship, the "Sparenryk". In honour of the occasion all the vessels in the harbour were decked with flags from sunrise to sunset, and a number of the highest officials were sent on board to take charge of the letter, which lay there in a silver tray covered with gold brocade. As they left the ship's side the crew manned the yards and raised three cheers, while the "Sparenryk" fired a salute of nineteen guns, which was taken up by all the other vessels. On landing a procession was formed which advanced between a double line of soldiers, under triumphal arches. A native regiment with colours flying led the way and was followed by drummers and trumpeters. Then came dragoons and grenadiers, with their colours and music, escorting the Disawa of Colombo, who carried the letter on his head. On either side of him walked two officers bearing lighted flambeaux; while washermen spread on the ground white linen on which the Disawa, and the bearers of the linen-covered case of presents which followed, should tread. Further grenadiers, dragoons and lascarins completed the escort.

The Governor, accompanied by the Council, awaited the procession at the gate of the Government House, where the Governor himself took charge of the letter and conveyed it, under a salute from the land battery and all the vessels in the harbour, within the reception room, where it was locked away in a special chest, which was guarded day and night by a dragoon and a lascarin with drawn swords, till its removal from Colombo.

In view of this attitude of the Company it was hardly to be expected that the Court would abate its claims. The tension was not relieved when in March 1762 the highborn Jan Lubert, Baron Van Eck, who had a reputation as a gallant soldier, replaced Schreuder; for he was not anxious to win unfamiliar honours on the field of diplomacy. While he was hurrying in all the soldiers who could be spared from India, the Court itself turned in the same direction for assistance. An application to the Nawab of the Carnatic was somewhat contemptuously refused, for, as he afterwards explained, the King was merely an *aldear* or country gentleman from Madura. On the other hand a verbal application to the Agents of the British Company at Fort St. George appeared to meet with a different reception, and on the 18th of May, Pybus, a member of the Council, appeared at Gannoruwa, having travelled by way of Kottiar. The diary kept by him during his visit has been preserved, and is full of interest as an authentic record of Court etiquette at the time.

Senkadagala Sriwardhana Pura was the official name of the capital which the Portuguese, confusing the capital with the principality—Kanda Uda Rata-- had generally described as Candia. Its position, situated as it was in a valley overshadowed by ranges of lofty hills, had naturally influenced its development. It consisted in the main of two streets each a mile in length, running North and South, and connected by cross streets. The Palace was towards the South, resting against the thick woods which were preserved as a place of refuge, and having a large enclosure on the North. The majority of the houses in the more important portion of the town were tiled, and built as they were at the foot of the hills, stood as a rule at a height of several feet above the streets. Every night at about 8 o'clock a bell was rung, and after that time no one could appear in the streets without a light.

Pybus was lodged at Gannoruwa at the *Tanayama* which was maintained there for the use of the

Company's ambassador. This consisted of a mudwalled and thatched house, built, according to the Sinhalese fashion, round an open square, containing many small apartments as well as stores for the presents which usually accompanied the embassy. In the middle of the square was a kind of shrine where the letter addressed to the King was kept under white cloth.

On the 24th Pybus was received in audience by the King. He started from the *Tanayama* at 7 p. m. amidst much firing of guns and beating of drums, the letter to the King, which rested in a silver tray between several folds of white linen, being carried in front of him under a silken canopy. Everybody went on foot, Pybus and the Minister who escorted him walking hand in hand; and it was not till half an hour before midnight that worn out and hungry, and bespattered with the mud which a heavy downfall of rain had caused, they arrived within sight of the Palace.

Here the procession halted till permission was received from the King to advance, which it did till it reached the outer gate of the Palace. Pybus was directed to stand there facing the gate till a Minister arrived to lead him in, when he took off his hat and entered. A second gateway led them into a square court-yard where some richly caparisoned horses and elephants were drawn up; Pybus now had to take off his shoes and was received by the Pallegampahe Adigar, who with many complimentary speeches led him into another court. Twelve halberdiers in white *Kabayas*, or long coats reaching to the knees, occupied this court, which led in turn to the Audience Hall, the entrance to which was concealed by a white curtain. Pybus now took the silver tray in his hands and raised it above his head, and then the curtain was drawn aside, revealing beyond it a second curtain of red.

Six curtains in succession were thus raised till a doorway was seen screened by another white curtain. At last this too was drawn aside and revealed the King seated on a handsomely carved gilt throne which stood on a dais three feet in height. He was dressed in a rich goldworked jacket worn over a close-fitting vest, with a broad gold-embroidered belt round his waist. On his head was a scarlet cap surmounted by a small jewelled crown; at his side was a jewelled dagger, while a large broad-sword with a jewelled handle rested against the throne. His feet were protected by slippers of crimson velvet and gold, and above him was suspended a canopy of white silk.

As soon as the last curtain was drawn aside, the courtiers prostrated themselves six times on the ground, at the same time invoking blessings on the King, who briefly responded to their salutation. Pybus remained standing with the tray on his head, till he was pulled down by the skirts of his coat and compelled to kneel on one knee. This ceremony was repeated four times, the party advancing by degrees till they reached the edge of a large Persian carpet which was spread in front of the throne. Pybus was then led up, and, kneeling on the lowest step of the dais, offered the letter to the King by whom it was received. He then stepped backwards to the edge of the carpet and knelt down again till he was given permission to sit down as was convenient to himself, which he was very glad to do.

The large dimly—lit hall in which the reception took place was entirely hung with white cloth, while ornamental arches adorned with ruffs of white and red cloth called *Reli-pallan* divided its length and formed aisles on either side. On each side of the hall sat three people holding in their hands the *Ran Awuda* or Golden Arms of the King; a narrow strip of cloth hung under their chins, and with these they covered their mouths whenever they had occasion to approach the throne. The conversation which followed was of a purely formal and complimentary nature.

The King's words were addressed to the Adigar, who knelt at the foot of the Throne; he prostrated himself and conveyed the question to one of the Disawas who was near Pybus. The Disawa in turn delivered it to a Malabar doctor who was in attendance, who addressed it in Tamil to Pybus' interpreter, who repeated it to Pybus in English. Every question which was put and every answer which was given were recorded immediately by a Secretary who was seated by a square stool on which a wax candle and writing materials were placed. At last the audience was finished, and the exhausted ambassador was permitted to withdraw, reaching the *tanayama* as the sun rose.

The negociations which followed led to nothing; this is hardly surprising, as the British Company had no intention whatever of assisting the King. Their instructions to Pybus were first to obtain permission to establish a settlement in Ceylon, and secondly to ascertain what concessions could be possibly forced out of the King. The courtiers however proved as expert as Pybus; they pointed out that the King had asked for British assistance, and they wanted to know what the price of that would be. Thereupon Pybus drew up a long statement of their demands, which, if conceded, would have given them the same privileges as the Hollanders enjoyed. After these demands had been duly considered, the question was put to Pybus whether, if they were complied with, the British would come to the assistance of the King; he was unable to give a definite reply, and there the matter ended, Pybus being sent back to his ship with all ceremony.

CHAPTER VIII.

In the meantime hostilities had not ceased. It was true that the Directors in Europe were earnestly anxious for peace and sent instructions accordingly, but van Eck was not suited for carrying through a delicate negociation. The King on his side would not lightly surrender the territory he had occupied, and war became inevitable. Chilaw and Puttalam were attacked by sea and occupied without much trouble, and in 1763 a large army started again for the mountains. With it there went a body of Moors who had been attracted by heavy pay and the promise of exemption from half the Uliyam or menial service which they had to render to the Company.

The whole expedition was mismanaged. The season was badly chosen; torrential rains rendered all advance through the forest belt a matter of extreme difficulty; little provision had been made for the conveyance of baggage and ammunition, or for maintaining the line of communications. The vanguard of the army did succeed in reaching the hills, only to be driven down with heavy loss. It fell back on the main army, but the condition of things was so hopeless that they were glad to beat a hurried retreat to Colombo.

The result was mortifying to the Hollanders, and the Sinhalese were exultant over this repetition of their success. While the Company was busy with the unfamiliar task of fighting, foreign merchants took the opportunity to encroach on its trade, and forty four of their vessels had been allowed entry in the course of twelve months. It was impossible to leave the disgrace unavenged, and very reluctantly the Directors gave their consent to a new expedition being prepared. All necessaries were brought over from Batavia; the Wannias of Katukulam Pattu and of Kottiar were won over to declare themselves on the side of the Company. Two hundred men occupied Venloos Bay against any assistance from outside; and the native levies were carefully organised.

In 1762 a more liberal spirit had been shewn in dealing with the Roman Catholics, and the legality of their baptisms and their right to marry before special Commissioners, had been recognised. As a consequence the priests exerted themselves to secure coolies for the proposed expedition, which some of them accompanied in person. Don Joan Illangakon, the inheritor of another great name, had been banished to the Cape for suspected complicity in the disturbances at Galle, but after two years the Batavian Government had directed his recall. His birth as well as his wealth, which was believed to be immense, gave him much influence, which van Eck was anxious to secure on the side of the Company. He therefore appointed Illangakon to be Field Maha Mudaliar, hoping that self interest at least would keep him faithful. The expedition was not regarded without some degree of despondency, and Don Simon Disanayaka, who was in charge of the Lascarins from Galle and Matara, made his Will before starting on the 2nd of December 1764, leaving his two swords and the gold chain which he had received from the King, to his three infant sons.

At last everything was ready, and on Sunday the 13th of January, 1765, van Eck set out from Colombo at the head of an army which included a large force of Malays. A second army started by way of Puttalam, and by the 12th of February the advanced guard, consisting of 1200 men including cavalry and artillery, drove the Sinhalese back and occupied Weuda. It was whispered about that the King had been betrayed by his Commanders; and soon after the Adigar and some other courtiers came and had an interview with van Eck. However, this did not check his advance. The Galagedera Pass which was defended by six batteries and a small fort of masonry, was occupied, and on the 16th of February the invading army pushing forward rapidly reached the Kingss' pleasure garden at Katugastota on the banks of the Mahaweli Ganga.

Repeated and urgent messages now arrived from the King, whose great anxiety was that the invaders should not enter his Captial. So delighted was van Eck with the success he had achieved that he wrote to Colombo to announce that the Kingdom was conquered, and that the defeated Sinhalese were compelled to beg for peace and receive it as a gift from the Company; he therefore requested that a special service of prayer and of thanksgiving to Almighty God for the favour he had shewn to the arms of the Company, might be held.

Indeed the King was prepared to make the most liberal concessions, if only his capital were not desecrated by a hostile occupation. Unfortunately the favourable terms he offered were not agreed to, for Johan Gerard van Angelbeek, the Political Secretary, urged the importance of re-establishing the prestige of the Company, which recent events so badly had tarnished. Acting on his advice van Eck insisted among other conditions that the king should pay a war indemnity of two hundred thousand pagodas, with an annual tribute of elephants, and that in addition he should lay down his crown and be crowned again as the vassal of the Company.

Needless to say these terms were rejected, and the King prepared to continue the struggle to the bitter end. The precious Tooth Relic guarded by its loyal attendants had already been removed to a place of safety. The King's brothers, with the Queens, their younger sister, and the most valuable of the royal treasures, disappeared into one of those mysterious hiding-places which were kept prepared for occasions of great emergency. It was not possible to take away the Company's officers who were prisoners, nor could they be permitted to rejoin their friends. In consequence the Captain of Matara was put to death, while the two other officers were allowed to shoot themselves. The King then withdrew to Hanguranketa, and the enemy crossed the river in spite of the advice of the military commander Colonel Feber.

Van Eck proceeded straight to the palace, where he established his headquarters.

This magnificent structure had been built in the last reign and three days were spent in sacking it. There was much booty consisting of gold and silver, precious stones and rich fabrics; and the wooden doors were stripped of the silver plates which covered them. The Company however obtained little benefit from all this wealth, which mainly went to enrich the officers. The Palace of Kundasala was next ransacked, and on the 24th nine hundred men were sent to Hanguranketa in pursuit of the King. They were in time only to see the Sinhalese disappearing over the mountains with their laden elephants, for the King had retreated to Badulla; thereupon they sacked and set fire to the Palace, after which they started to return.

The Sinhalese however had been patiently watching; every passage and pathway was beset; from every thicket arrows and bullets came flying from an unseen foe; and soon the Hollanders were reduced to a disorderly rabble fleeing for their lives. At last half dead of fatigue and hunger and with heavy loss they reached their headquarters, and van Eck realised that he had committed a grievous mistake. He accordingly sent three messages in succession to the King, offering to accept the terms which the King had proposed, but his letters were returned unread. In the meantime everything was done to devastate the country. Everything with life that bore the name of Sinhalese was killed; everything that could be set on fire was burnt; and whatever could be destroyed was destroyed. The temples in the neighbourhood of the Capital were the special objects of the enemy's greed; fortunately the priests headed by the Sangha Raja had escaped in time, taking with them their precious books and relics.

The Sinhalese would not be coerced; not a symptom of surrender could be seen. Sickness, which in the past had so often proved a staunch ally, again came to their assistance, and on the 4th of March Van Eck was glad to start back for Colombo. The Sacred Tooth was beyond his reach, but he took with him, as memorials of his Pyrrhic victory, the large silver *Karanduwa* which formed its outermost covering, as well as the gold howdah in which it was usual to convey it in procession. His retreat, for such it had become, was not carried out without much trouble. The roads were infested by bands of hostile Sinhalese, but fortunately Dassanayaka, the Mudaliyar of the Hapitigam Korale, knew of a secret track by which the Hollanders were able to escape into the Seven Korales.

Van Eck left behind him a garrison of 1800 men under the command of de Feber, pending the arrival of Marten Rein, once a tailor, who had been appointed Commandant. On the 28th de Feber himself set out for Colombo and on the road he received the news that Van Eck, who had been very depressed since his return, had suddenly died; it was believed by many that he had killed himself in despair.

To the Sinhalese the mystery of this unhappy end to a promising career was not difficult to understand. "There fell upon that most foolish leader of the enemy's hosts a fearful and terrible madness that was brought about by the power of the gods and also by the power of the King's Merit, so that he abandoned that fine city and left it ingloriously and was consumed by the fire of Death. And all the enemy's hosts who had come under the leadership of that foolish man became powerless and helpless and were overtaken by calamities. Some fell victims to disease, others suffered great distress from famine and sickness, some were slain in battle, and others betook themselves to mountain fastnesses. Thus were these enemies, the vilest of men, destroyed and put to flight."

Such is the stately narrative of the writer of the Mahawansa.

Matters were looking very grave; the Sinhalese appeared to be in every place, and as Feber retired he withdrew the garrisons on the line of communication as far as Wisinawaya, thus leaving Rein and his men isolated in the heart of the enemy's country. These were ill provisioned and soon found themselves completely blockaded; it was realised at Colombo that their position was extremely critical, and it was not possible to communicate with them by letter. Rein himself was seriously ill, the monsoon rains were close at hand, and by the 11th of April the exasperated Sinhalese had come as far as the boundary at Sitawaka, wreaking their vengence on everyone and everything which belonged to the Company.

Plans were prepared to relieve Rein by the ill-omened route through the Balane Pass, and urgent messages were sent to the aged Anthony Moyaart, who was at Jafanapatnam, to come and take charge of affairs at Colombo. Hostilities however did not cease, and the beleaguered garrison was being steadily killed off by disease and lack of food, for the Sinhalese realised that it was not necessary for them to incur any risk.

In August Iman Willem Falck arrived as Governor; he was at the time only twenty nine years of age, having been born in Colombo in 1736, while his mother, the daughter of a Governor of Malaca, was a native of Samarang. The young *casti* whose swarthy complexion earned for him the sobriquet of The Crow, had received an excellent education at Utrecht, and it was soon clear that he was one of the ablest Administrators the Company had yet sent to Ceylon. The difficult situation was taken firmly in hand; negociations were entered into with the Court; and on the 10th of August a concialtory letter was sent to the Ministers. Arrangements were made for a display of military force on various parts of the frontiers; and rumours were spread abroad that the Company intended to dethrone the King, and that his successor had already been selected and entrusted to the care of the Governor. At the same time efforts were made to secure the sympathy of the inhabitants of the coast, and in October Dassanayaka, who had probably saved Van Eck and his escort from destruction, was presented with a medal and chain as an expression of the Company's gratitude, and allowed four drummers as a mark of distinction.

Fortunately for his designs the prolonged hostilities had seriously interrupted the cultivation of the fields in the King's territory, and his subjects were on the verge of starvation. In December an Ambassador came from the King, and Falck increased the pressure he had brought to bear. All the stores of salt were searched out and destroyed; while the Three, Four, and Seven Korales were ravaged from end to end. The garrison of Trincomalee advanced into the Bintenne; another force under Major Duflo occupied Matale, where people were found to be dying of starvation. A palace which the King had in that district was burnt to the ground; a store of 15,000 bags of saltpetre, which had been patiently collected for many years from the deposits of bats, was found in a cave and destroyed.

The people were utterly exhausted, and among the Ministers themselves discontent was noticeable. Falck now adopted a conciliatory attitude, and sent back the great *Karanduwa* and the golden howdah to the King. These tactics proved effective, the scanty remnants of the garrison were allowed to return to Colombo, and five Commissioners headed by Dumbara Rala arrived from Court to discuss the terms of peace. The ragged condition of their attendants, who carefully saved everything which they could out of the provisions supplied to them by the Company, proved how extreme was the pitch of want to which the King's subjects had been reduced. The negociations were conducted by Van Angelbeek and Godfried Leonard de Coste, the able Disawa of Colombo, on behalf of the Company; and after much wrangling the draft of a new Treaty was signed at Colombo at 7.30 p. m. on the 14th of February 1766.

By this agreement, which contained twenty five Articles, the Company was ackowledged as sovereign over the districts it had possessed previous to the commencement of the war. Moreover the King ceded to it the whole of the seaborde which had remained to him, for the distance of a *gowwa* inland, the Company undertaking to pay him yearly the revenue which was collected therefrom. He was acknowledged paramount over the rest of the Island, and all other territory occupied by the Company during the war was to be restored to him. The right to take as much salt as they liked from the Lewayas, Puttalam, and Chilaw, was reserved for his subjects, while the Company obtained the privilege of peeling cinnamon from the whole of the Low Countries belonging to the King, namely, Sabaragamuwa, and the Three, Four, and Seven Korales, as far as Balane. The cinnamon found east of Balane was to be peeled by the King's subjects and sold at a fixed rate exclusively to the Company, which obtained in addition the monopoly of the trade in ivory, pepper, cardamons, coffee, arecanuts, and wax.

There was to be unrestricted trade between the subjects of the two contracting parties, with the right of entry into each others, territory for the purpose, the Company undertaking to procure for the King such articles as he required from foreign countries. In return he agreed to supply the Company at Batticaloa and Trincomalee with all the timber they needed, and to surrender all the Hollanders who were kept as prisoners by him, together with the cannon captured at Hanwella. There was also provision for the restoration of runaway slaves, and the extradition of criminals.

The Company pledged itself to protect the King's dominions from all external aggression, and to make no agreement with any foreign power which might be prejudicial to him ; while the King promised not to enter into any treaty with any other European power or Indian Prince, and to deliver up all Europeans coming within his territory. The humiliating ceremonial which the Company's ambassadors up till now had been compelled to go through when received in audience, was at last abolished, and for the future the same ceremonies were to be observed at such receptions on either side.

Till the very last there was fear that the negociations would break down; the parties could not agree as to whose name should have precedence, but a compromise was arrived at by which it was settled that the name of each party should be placed first in the copy to be retained by that party. The Sinhalese pressed for the exchange of all captured guns and deserters, but the Hollanders refused to agree; the more so as it was traitors from among the King's subjects who had acted as guides for their army. The Sinhalese translation of the treaty was prepared by Illangakon and the Predicant Philipsz, and was examined word for word by the Commissioners; the original, which was to be signed by the King, was engrossed on gilt parchment.

Falck made a confidential suggestion to the Commissioners that a clause should be inserted excluding all Malabars from office within the Kingdom; the Commissioners expressed their delight at the suggestion but said that the time was not yet ripe for carrying it out; they significantly added that they thought it would come soon if they could rely on the assistance of the Company. Falck also ascertained from them that there was a strong secret party at Court which supported the pretensions of a certain Prince of Kilakarai to the Sinhalese throne; he was a son of the sister of Kundasala's Queens, and asserted that his mother too had been married to that King.

The day following the signature of the draft the Commissioners started back accompanied by de Coste, who was delegated to obtain the King's ratification. Duflo was ordered to withdraw from Matale, which he was glad to do, as every European with him was sick.

The King signed the treaty at Hanguranketa. A request was made by de Coste that it should be countersigned by the Ministers, but this was peremptorily refused: the King's signature was all-sufficient, and the treaty of Batticaloa which was produced, bore the signature of Raja Sinha alone. De Coste returned to Colombo with the perfected document and a tusked elephant which the King had presented to him. He was followed by a letter in which the King protested that it was only his love of peace which induced him to sign an agreement so inequitable as the present Treaty; he complained of the loss of his sea-coast, and the refusal to return his guns and deserting subjects, and declared that further representations would be made to Batavia on the subject.

The long-cherished policy of the Company was at last achieved, and the King cut off from all foreign intercourse. His Kingdom was now dependent for everything which could not be produced locally, on the humour of the Company's officials, and the trade of his subjects had to be regulated by its demands. But this success was not purchased cheap. It was calculated by Burnand, a Swiss who was one of the most distinguished servants of the Company, that the war had cost ten million florins and some thousands of lives; it had dislocated its trade, and greatly retarded the progress of cultivation; but above all it had roused the hatred of the Court and rendered necessary the maintenance of a military force which swallowed up a great part of the revenue. However for the moment the Company's prospects appeared to be bright, and it was able to settle the troublesome questions affecting South India which had been a source of anxiety for a long time.

Even before the arrival of van Gollenesse there had been disagreements with the Thever, and the Company had been forced to pull down its factory at Kilakarai. The quarrel, which was largely connected with the question of the smuggling of areca, was patched up about 1747, and the factory was restored. Eleven years later the Thever again attacked the factory and seized the Company's vessels on his coast, and the embarrassments of Schreuder were increased by these hostilities, which were however concluded in March 1759 by the restoration of what had been seized. Falck was fortunate enough to find a child ruling in Ramnad, and on the 24th of January 1767, he entered into an agreement with Thamotharam Pillai, the Thever's Guardian and Regent, by which the Pamben passage was sold to the Company, subject to the right of the Thever's people to its unrestricted use.

Two successful fisheries gave Falck a good chance for restoring order in Ceylon after the unrest created by the late war. The first step was to organise some kind of administration in the newly acquired districts. The boundary near Chilaw was cleared and marked by a series of stout posts bearing the Company's device. Orders were given to strengthen the wretched little fort at the town, and to repair the great irrigation bunds of the Sinhalese; for the reputation of its rich fields was such that dhonies used to come to Chilaw from Kalutara and Welitara to obtain rice. There were valuable pepper gardens belonging to the King, which were now taken over on account of the Company. Udupenkarai, once the chief nest of the smugglers, was an important fishing centre which supplied the bulk of the Sinhalese Kingdom with salt fish, and good tobacco was produced to the north of Kaymel. At Chilaw itself the majority of the inhabitants were fishers; they were divided into two rival factions, and by ancient custom one supplied the chief official at the fort with river fish in the morning, and the other with sea fish in the evening. The distinction was maintained even in the *ranchus* of Lascarins which were raised among them.

In Puttalam there were few Sinhalese; the majority of the inhabitants were Moors, while the Mukkuwas, who had settled there before the Moors, ranked next in number, and were either nominal Christians, or Mohammedans. The chiefs of the district were Wannias, who were believed to be Mukkuwas by race. There were originally twelve of them who formed a *Rata Sabhawa* presided over by the Kanakapulle and the Vidane appointed by the King's Disawa. The office of Wannia was hereditary, and the lands belonging to them were exempt from Rajakariya, while they were entitled to certain duties from the crops of the villagers. They had no special jurisdiction of their own, but were expected to inquire into and settle small disputes. Falck called upon these Wannias and the chief Moormen to prepare a statement of the customs which prevailed in the country, and directed that the Landraad which he now established should administer justice in accordance with them. Criminal offences were to be punished according to the Sinhalese practice.

The most important industry in the district was the production of salt, chiefly for consumption within the Kingdom, while fishing, both in the lake and on the high seas, afforded a means of livelihood to many. Eight dhonies were employed on the former branch, and there were well-defined rules regulating the privilege of casting their nets, etc. The deep-sea fish was usually salted and dried, while the rest was used for immediate consumption. There was a fair local production of cotton, and much rough cloth was woven by the women. The Commandant at Puttalam received various perquisites from the *tavalams,* salt, arrack rent and judicial fines.

On the eastern side of the Island a Landraad was established at Batticaloa where there was also a Council of Chiefs similar to that of the Wannias at Puttalam. A tribute of elephants was levied from various petty chiefs, including some of those of Tamankaduwa, who had for the time joined the Company. Great hopes were entertained of the possibilities of Batticaloa, with its rich soil and industrious population, but Falck realised, as van Goens had pointed out in 1671, that the fort should have been built not on Puliyandivu but further south where there was a safe coast and deep water. The old fort of Kottiar was now of little value, while the increasing power of the British in India made the protection of the inner harbour of Trincomalee a matter of urgency.

At Jaffna the weary task of strengthening the fort was still going on in accordance with a scheme devised by a certain Brohier; in consequence the Uliam service to which the people were liable had been doubled, and yet but little progress was made; for the Tamil man working under compulsion knew very well how to produce the minimum of result in the maximum of time. There was also difficulty about the supply of lime and stone, though the stratum of rock which lay under the moat was blown up with powder to supply the necessary material. It was to the interest of the Commandeur to encourage the export of palmyrah timber, and consequently there was still great anxiety as to the effect of the felling of the trees on the food supply of the people.

Schreuder had proposed to drain the Uppu Aru in Jaffna and bring it under cultivation, and with this object he had caused a survey to be made; the scheme however was abandoned in view of the unfavourable opinion expressed by some of the authorities consulted. At Colombo de Coste devoted himself to the improvement of the great tract of Mutu raja wela, estimated to contain 6000 acres, the value of which as likely to ensure a sufficiency of rice for Colombo, was long recognised by the Company. An attempt which had been made by it to improve the existing Sinhalese canal had led to the inundation of the land by salt water and the fields now lay waste. De Coste set about dealing with this problem as well as the overflow into the tract from the rivers, and the stagnation of water. He built a series of dams, sluices and channels, and was so far successful in his efforts that in 1767 he was able to announce that the work was complete, and the Governor ordered the division of the area into allotments and the appointment of a special Head of the Cultivation. Under him were placed twelve Goi Vidanes, who were provided with silver-headed canes as a badge of office. The cost of the improvements was to be met by a second tythe on the crops. But in a few years the scheme was found to be a failure, and the land was again abandoned.

A canal was opened to connect Negumbo with the Maha Oya, and in 1771 another was opened from Kotte to the Moratuwa Lake by way of Nedimale. The completion of this latter was celebrated by the presentation of a medal to Daniel Alwis Samarasinha, the energetic Mudaliyar of the Salpiti Korale, who was mainly responsible for the work. Both these canals had to be cleaned and deepened yearly by a certain number of service tenants. The necessity for permitting the clearing of *henas* in those Korales where the rice fields were less fertile was recognised, and this cultivation was permitted though under stringent conditions. No *hena* could be cleared without special permission, and before the permission was granted the land had to be inspected by Commissioners assisted by Chalias, and it would be refused if six peelable cinnamon plants were found within the extent of a *morgen.* Wild cinnamon grew in abundance where a land was once sown, and therefore the same spot would not be cleared oftener then once in fifteen or twenty years. The cultivation of *Amu* was forbidden, as this grain was considered harmful to cinnamon. Hena crops paid a duty of a tenth to the Company.

There had been bitter complaints about the regulations for the protection of cinnamon growing on private lands, which compelled the people to leave valuable cultivated lands uncleared. A Commission was appointed to inquire into the matter and permission was given to clear such lands provided the cinnamon found growing on them was not damaged in the process. The expectations that had been formed of an increase in the supply of cinnamon as a consequence of the new Treaty were doomed to disappointment, for the King was not prepared to take any trouble to have the stuff collected in his dominions for the small price that the Company was willing to pay, and the supply rapidly decreased.

Falck accordingly attempted to cultivate the plant, and his first experiment, which was carried out in the Maradana of Colombo in 1769, was so successful that all native headmen were directed to open similar gardens, a medal being promised to the most successful. Samarasinha again distinguished himself and received the coveted honour, while Wikramasinha of Negumbo was presented with a silver sword and created a Mudaliyar.

CHAPTER IX

The Disawa continued to fill a large space in the eye of the villager. The Disawa of Colombo called himself Maha Disawa of Sabaragamuwa, the Seven Korales, and Low Country of Colombo, and was escorted in his circuits through his district by a *ranchu* of Lascarins under an Arachchi, with its colours, five drums, a horn and a trumpet. He and the Commandeurs of Galle and Jaffna alone were entitled to have their drums beaten within the *Kadawatu* of Colombo, as far as Kayman's Gate on the one side, and Kollupitiya on the other, and within the Castle he was allowed an escort of six Lascarins. In addition to his salary and table allowance, he held the important Gabadagama of Mahara, and also received certain fines, a percentage on gratuities paid to certain public servants, and free provisions when on circuit. When the Commission of a new Governor was read to the public he received an entertainment allowance of seventy-two bottles of sack, one barrel of beer, and 190 cans of "double arrack" from the Company's garden at Galkissa, with a proportion of sugar, beef, bacon, spices, and wheat. His duties were as multifarious as formerly; for instance no Mohammedan could marry without his licence, under pain of being put in chains.

The superior headmen who were under him, namely the Mudaliyars, Koralas, Maha Vidanes, and Mohundirams, were appointed under the hand of the Governor; but, as in the time of the Sinhalese Kings, the petty headmen received their appointments from the Disawa, and he had authority to punish them even with a whip or rattan or by putting them in chains. This extreme power had to be exercised cautiously; as the experienced de Coste pointed out in 1770, "He should take care not to abuse them in a passion in the presence of the people, much less beat them, for by such treatment they lose the respect of their inferiors, and the Disawa himself is despised by the natives, who from nature abhor all passionate persons." As a rule a Disawa held office for a term of five years.

The Company had deliberately set itself to destroy the power of the Mudaliyars, and as a general rule they had fallen much from their original position, and their military responsibilities been largely replaced by administrative duties. They had to see to the disposal of the Lascarins under their charge among the various guard stations, supervise the removal of timber felled on account of the Company, and repair school buildings. They also assisted at the elephant hunt which was held in the Alut Kuru Korale, attended to the proper cultivation of their districts, and provided *Adukku* and *pehidun* for ambassadors, and officials, including clergymen, on circuit. In time of war they supplied men for the conveyance of ammunition. Some of the Mudaliyars were men of wealth and great influence, and in consequence were jealously watched by the Company. A new register of Lascarins had been recently prepared and an effort made to reduce the number of these men, who had little work to do in time of peace. The duty of Kodituwakku bearers was abolished, and the Kodituwakku men were expected to carry the guns in future. This caused much discontent, for to carry loads was considered a degrading task; but the sympathy with which the prejudices of the natives had once been regarded was fast disappearing.

Their discontent was ascribed to a false pride, in the same way as their jealousy with respect to the honours of the white cloth. The fixed policy now was to destroy all this kind of feeling, to tear the people away from their past, to denationalise them as much as possible: it might have been all right to uphold these customs so long as it was considered necessary to flatter and hoodwink the natives, but that time was over, and they must now learn that their chief mission in life was to secure dividends for the Company. "Common sense directs" said de Coste, "that all these country pomps and grandeurs should be abolished, in order to remove from the natives the impression that the customs of the Sinhalese and their Kings are much more venerable than ours."

The manner in which natives were to dress at their feasts was regulated by Placaat. People who were bound to perform duty to the Company in consequence of their castes often adopted European dress and passed as Burghers in order to escape the liability, and it was therefore enacted that no person would be exempted unless he produced a Burgher Act, written upon a stamped paper. Women of the seven highest castes alone were entitled to wear jackets; they could also freely adorn themselves with jewels; but those who had to serve in the houses of Goigama people were expected to be restrained in their use so as to avoid giving offence.

The Nanayakkara and Nambukara Appuhamis of the Goigama caste ranked as noble, while the Safframado Appuhamis, who frequently were nominated by the Mudaliyars, were employed to mount guard at the Governor's and the Disawa's *Wasala* and bore the canopy under which ambassadors went in procession. The fisher people of Negombo and Kalutara were liable to the duty of loading and unloading vessels, and those of Moratuwa and Panadura were attached to the carpenters' and cartwrights' establishments. The village blacksmith, barber, and washerman could cause as much annoyance to the Appuhami by refusing to perform their essential services, as they still do to the Wellala of Jaffna. Potters from places so remote as the Hapitigam Korale had to work at the Company's brick kiln near Kelaniya, but they were paid for their labour.

In Colombo there were licensed cockpits, the birds employed being as a rule fitted with metal spurs: cockfighting was greatly in favour with the Malays, with their strong instinct for gambling; in the rural districts people were allowed on occasions of festivity to have cockpits in their own gardens. In consequence of the increasing number of robberies and murders, a Placaat was passed to the effect that trespassers found after nightfall within enclosed land were liable to be shot dead. The duties of undertakers at funerals, the manner in which relatives were to be summoned on such occasions, and the number of mourning cloaks and hat bands which could be used, were as much a matter of regulation, as the question of whether a barber's daughter might or might not wear stockings when she got married. After 1769 the sale of firearms and ammunition was placed under severe restrictions.

In matters of religion a more tolerant attitude, the result in part of indifference and in part of necessity, had begun to appear, and there was no longer any interference with the worship of the Buddhists at Kelaniya, Attanagalla and Warana. Mulgirigala still retained its ancient sanctity and was visited by Falck more than once. He was broad-minded enough to see the necessity of understanding the religious views of the people of the country, and he invited the priests to enlighten him on the subject. In the case of the Mohammedans religion and law are closely connected, and Falck had a statement prepared of the customs of the Moors with regard to inheritance, and directed that they should be observed as law. As for the Roman Catholics, the Goanese influence continued to be so great that he expressed the opinion that it must be destroyed somehow, and he agreed that in order to secure this desirable end, Protestant natives should receive the preference in appointments to office. This really made little difference, for the bulk of the native chiefs were secretly staunch Buddhists, while the caste distinctions observed even by those who professed Christianity made them insist on separate places of worship being provided for themselves.

In the North the Tamils were not worried any longer for being Hindus, provided they did not openly maintain temples or hold religious processions. An account of the condition of things among them has been left by Johannes Christophel Wolfs, the son of a humble German tradesman of Mecklenburg, who succeeded in making his way into Ceylon in 1749 as a youth of nineteen years. He remained in the country for nearly twenty years more, the greater portion of his time being spent in Jaffnapatnam, where his perseverance, discretion, and capacity for bearing without a murmur the kicks and cuffings of his superiors, secured him rapid promotion in the service of the Company. In 1782, after his return to his own country, he published in German a brief account of his experiences.

He always regarded with sympathy the Tamils, at whose hands he had received much simple kindness in his days of obscurity, and whose language he strove to learn; indeed he was one of the few European writers who understood the people sufficiently to have a good word to say for them. They still dressed in the primitive style of their ancestors, both men and women as a rule being bare above the waist, though people of quality would throw a piece of linen over their shoulders. The long distended ear-lobes, which had nearly disappeared among the Sinhalese, were sedulously cultivated, and caste distinctions rigidly maintained.

That petty family vanity which so frequently characterises small and isolated communities and is still so marked a feature of Tamil life, was turned by the Company to good advantage. The equivalent of a patent of nobility, signified by the tying of a silver *nalalpata*, and the conferring of the title of Don, could always be purchased from it at a moderate sum, which Wolfs declares finally sank as low as ten rix dollars. Every Wellala who could afford the money got himself ennobled, and this gave the opportunity to the Brahmins, their rivals, to expose their pretensions to public ridicule. The result was much quarrelling and litigation.

The father was the autocrat of his family; the marriage arrangements which he made for his son had to be acquiesced in without question, under risk of disinherison. To secure a husband for a daughter or a sister was the first duty of a citizen, and with that object often the bulk of the property would be given to the daughters by way of dowry. Such dowry could not be touched for the father's debts, which then fell on the sons, though impatience was being displayed at what was considered an inequitable rule. Large powers of adoption were vested in the head of a family.

From the point of view of missionary enterprise the Tamils were frankly recognised as being merely baptised heathen. The clergyman visited the parishes once a year, but only to marry, baptise, and check the school registers, while the bulk of the Churches were abandoned or used as cattle stalls. There was the same desire for schooling as still distinguishes the Tamil boy, and his powers of memory and mastery over figures were as much remarked by Wolfs as the calfless legs of the men. The schoolmasters acted as Notaries, drawing up all formal deeds, and preserving copies thereof. The Brahmins burnt their dead and buried the ashes in a pot, while the other Tamils interred the bodies in shallow graves in the Churchyards, without coffins and merely wrapped in a sheet.

In the meanwhile with the conclusion of peace the King had returned to his Capital. Those who had served him faithfully during the war were rewarded generously, while the treacherous Moors who had repaid the hospitality which they had received in his country by assisting the enemy, were expelled from several districts. He next sent four ambassadors, including Kapuwatta and the brave Palingupana, to Batavia to represent to the authorities there his objections to the recent treaty; they were given a very ceremonious reception, but could obtain no modification of the terms. Both Kapuwatta and Palingupana died on the return journey, and a diamond ring which had been presented to the former was submitted to the King. He thereupon ordered the gem to be set on the forehead of the beautiful jewelled Bird ornament which was being prepared as an offering to the Sacred Tooth, in order that Kapuwatta might reap the Merit thereof.

He now turned with passionate enthusiasm to the encouragement of religion. First and foremost the Tooth Relic had to be restored to its proper place in the new Maligawa which he had built for it by the side of his Palace. For three years it had remained concealed within the cave at Kevulgama, in the charge of Rambukwelle Unanse and its faithful hereditary attendants. And now the *Karanduwa* which the touch of the enemy had defiled was gilded with refined gold and set with gems, the whole city was cleaned and purified, and once more, with the most impressive solemnity and all the pomp which the kingdom could display, the precious Relic was brought back on the head of the King and reinstalled within its shrine.

There it continued to be the object of his ceaseless adoration ; nothing that could give pleasure to the mind of man or add to the dignity of its surroundings, was refused to this emblem of his people. The sweetest smelling flowers, the most fragrant of ripe fruit, the daintiest food; gold and silver and precious stones, horses and elephants, men servants and maid servants, with rich villages, were offered to it with a lavish hand. It was not the desire of the King that the happiness and Merit of adoring the Relic should be stinted or confined to a few; more than once the solemn mystery which surrounded it was brushed aside and it was exposed to the public gaze, held aloft in his own hand on its lotus of gold.

Gangarama Vihare, which the King had built and Van Eck destroyed, was restored with great splendour; a new Vihare was erected at Kundasala; Ridi Vihare, which Dutugemunu had founded, was rebuilt on a scale of grandeur; and throughout the length and breadth not only of his own Kingdom but also of the whole of the Island, the zeal of the King made itself felt.

This was a source of no little anxiety to the Company, for all the Nayaka or Chief Priests within its territory went to Court to receive their appointments as such from the King, and in consequence they were his warm supporters. The influence which they exercised over the most powerful Mudaliyars was known to be great, and therefore it was found necessary to keep a strict watch over the latter, while at the same time cultivating the good-will of the former.

The school which the Sangha Raja had gathered round him zealously pursued the study of Pali, and many books dealing with the subject were produced. Attaragama Bandara, the best known of his lay pupils, is still quoted as an authority. Tibbatuwawa was entrusted by the King with the task of collating the Sinhalese versions of the Mahawansa with a copy received from Siam, and bringing the narrative up to date from the records of his Court. Accounts were compiled of the various missions which had been sent to Siam, and a *Katikawata* or Code of Rules was prepared for the guidance of the conduct of the priesthood. Moratota, one of the Sangha Raja's pupils, was appointed Tutor to the King's brother, who afterwards mounted the Throne as Raja Adhiraja Sinha; the royal student proved an apt pupil and obtained much applause by his work, the Asadrisa Jatakaya. The Sangha Raja died in 1778; a small *dagoba* at Ampitiya enshrines his ashes, while the story of his life was recorded in verse by Munkotuwe Rala, at the request of Moratota. This work is the Sangharaja Vata, and was completed in 1782. The only other literary figure of interest at Court was Dunuwila Gajanayaka Nilame, who was the author of some clever erotic verse, as well as of the Dunuwila Hatane.

This revival of literature within the Kingdom was accompanied by a similar and more fruitful movement in the South under the inspiration of Sitinamaluwe Dammajoti of Wehelle, the author of a valuable commentary on the Balawatara. Matara still contained great families like the Ekanayakas, Tennekons and Illangakons, willing to play the part of the generous Maecenas. Some members of these families were themselves no mean scholars; they, as the Hollanders so frequently complained, were educated at home by Buddhist priests, through whose means the literary influence of the Sangha Raja made itself felt. Tilakaratna Mudaliyar, grandson of the renegade Punchi Appuhami, compiled a valuable work known as the Bhesajja Nidana, while in 1768 Disanayaka Mudaliyar wrote his Makaraddaja.

Poetical works of great skill, based on the Jataka stories, were produced by priests, such as Dhammananda of Kirambe. They show exceptional polish in preparation and skill in technique, but suffer from a defect which runs through all later Sinhalese art. The poet felt himself constrained to follow certain venerable conventions, and sacrificed originality in displaying scholarship. The test of good poetry was not only whether it was marked by those graces which are considered such in all languages, but also whether those charms were expressed in certain set forms dictated by ancient canons, which no one had the courage to set at defiance.

In Sinhalese poetry, while rich imagery, choice language and melody of sound were keenly appreciated and artistically used, there were also other ornaments which appealed to the intellect of the curious and received perhaps an exaggerated degree of admiration. The best exponent of these latter was Samarajiwa Pattayame Lekama, a dissipated genius, whose amatory poems published in 1768 brought him into great reputation. Two years later Samarasekera of Katuwana produced the Kav Mini Maldama, a poem based on a Jataka story, which takes rank amongst the first order of later Sinhalese poetry. The invocation to Saraswati, Patroness of the Arts, which opened the poem so offended the vain Illangakon, to whom the poet had presented a copy, that he curtly referred the writer to the goddess for his expected reward. Samarajiwa hastened to take advantage of the Maha Mudaliyar's displeasure by offering to him his Kav Mini Kondala, a work also based on a Jataka story and sparkling with brilliant *jeux d' esprit.* For instance his alliterations consist not only of letters, but of syllables, words, and even of entire lines, as when a verse is formed of the same line repeated four times, each repetition bearing a different meaning. Verse after verse rhymes not only at the end of the lines but also at the middle. In certain couplets the second half of the line is formed by writing the first half backwards. The works of the Pattayame Lekama are a store-house of these ingenious devices.

The Kav Mutu Hara of Maniratna of Saliella, written in 1784 as a memorial to a child of the

Ekanayaka family, also is based on a Jataka story and belongs to the best work of the period. Barana Ganitaya who wrote the Nilakobo Sandesaya, yet another of that group of poems which followed on the lines of the Mega Dhuta; and Gajaman Nona, the best known poetess among the Sinhalese, complete the list of the chief writers of the Matara school in the eighteenth century.

Besides the poetic devices mentioned above, metrical puzzles were much in favour. These were formed by arranging letters in diagrams which could be read in various directions. Perhaps the most famous of these was the Baranama Gabasaka, which was formed by Karatota Dhammarama Unanse of Weragampita. This priest had a reputation for learning and was consulted by Governor Falck for information regarding Buddhism, and he was also considered an authority on astronomy. The Gabasaka consisted of a Diagram which when read in the four directions formed sixteen elaborately polished verses in praise of the Buddha. This was presented in 1786 to Raja Adhiraja Sinha and the ingenious author was rewarded by the gift of the vast desolation of Pallebeddegama in the Atakalan Korale.

The Company's yearly embassies to the Court still continued, though the ambassadors were no longer expected to go through all the humiliating antics to which Pybus had been subjected; and in 1769 it assisted to convey the King's fourth Queen to the Island from India. In the meantime it was exposed to a new unpleasantness; for the powerful Nawab of the Carnatic, who had reduced the Thever and was supported by the British, was advancing a claim to a share in the Pearl Fishery. The Company was indignant, but was not in a position to give effect to its indignation, and entered into long haggling negociations, without in any way persuading the Nawab to abate his demands.

It is not improbable that the King received secret encouragement from the same quarter, for it was well known that the British still had their eyes fixed on the Island; and he appears to have sent an embassy to Tanjore in 1772. At any rate in 1775 a request was received from the Court for a share of the Fishery, and the demand was renewed the next year with a further request for the restoration of a portion of the coast. Both demands were sharply refused.

The Company had not kept its agreement to allow the Sinhalese free access to the salt pans, in a liberal spirit. For two hundred years the control of the salt supply had been an object on which the Europeans on the coast had set their hearts, and the Company having at last secured it was determined to put it to the best use possible. It was true the Sinhalese were allowed to remove the salt, but they were not permitted to take away more than was just sufficent for their current needs, for fear that they would store it up in their country. To prevent this the bulk of the salt which was formed used to be thrown back into the sea.

Successive bad harvests in the North, which reduced the people of Jaffna to the verge of famine, increased the troubles of the Company. Moreover the Wanniyas had become gradually more and more independent and defiant in their attitude, till at last nothing could be done in the Wanni without their consent. The Company therefore resolved to bring the district under its direct administration, and Lieutenant Nagel, who had previous experience at Manar, was entrusted with the task. This was not accomplished without much trouble, especially from the adherents of two Wannichchis, Nella Nachchi and Chinna Nachchi. The former of these had been placed in 1765 over the important division of Panangaman in succession to her mother's brother Don

Gaspar Nalla Mapane, who had been removed from office three years before on a charge of disobedience. Chinna Nachchi fled to the King but returned not long after and settled down at Mullaitivu, while the Wanni was handed over to Nagel to be administered on his own account, subject to the payment of an yearly tribute in rice to the Company. He was allowed to maintain a small military force for Police purposes, and his administration of this desolate region was considered a success. He left behind an important report on the history and resources of the district.

In the meantime war broke out between England and her American Colonies which in February 1778 entered into an offensive and defensive alliance with France. They were soon joined by Spain, and a quarrel with the Netherlands on the question of the right of search threw the fleet of the latter into the scale against England. The struggle spread to India and the Company, which under its constitution was responsible for the protection of its territory, was obliged to hire three regiments of mercenaries from Europe at a ruinous rate. It was, however, too late and the Company's factories in the Southern coast were rapidly captured. In November 1781 Nagapatnam fell, and then the British fleet under the command of Sir Edward Hughes proceeded to Trincomalee, where it arrived on the 4th of January 1782.

The importance of fortifying this valuable harbour had long been pressed on the Company, which could never bring itself to sanction the necessary expenditure. The result was that Trincomalee was captured without trouble, and Fort Ostenburg with its garrison of four hundred men surrendered in a couple of days.

The plan of the British was to capture Colombo as soon as possible, and by cutting off the Company's cinnamon trade, to compel it to surrender all its territory. If the weather did not permit of vessels sailing to Colombo, their intention was to occupy Jaffna, as being the second place of importance in the Island. It was expected that the King would render gladly any assistance he could in the hope of getting back what he had lost in 1766, and with the fleet there had come as ambassador to the Court a certain Hugh Boyd, a brilliant but impecunious Irishman, who was at one time believed to be the author of the Letters of Junius, and who had come out as second Secretary to Lord Macartney, the new Governor of Madras. On the 5th of February Boyd set out from Trincomalee with a long train of followers, but before that date the King had died.

Kirti Sri was fond of horses, and proud of his skill in managing them ; he was riding through the streets of his Capital on a spirited animal which the Hollanders had presented to him, when he met with a serious accident which after some months of suffering, ended fatally. As he left no children by his *Ran doli*, he was succeeded on the throne by his younger brother with the name of Raja Adhiraja Sinha.

Boyd's mission ended in failure. It was true that the new King was persuaded with much difficulty to agree to supply the British forces with provisions, but the Ministers, after their experience with Pybus, refused to discuss the question of a treaty of alliance, or of hostilities against the Company, save with an ambassador authorised by the King of England himself. Boyd, finding that nothing was likely to be gained by further delay, therefore started back for his ship. In the meantime Hughes, who had returned to Madras for provisions leaving behind a garrison at Trincomalee, had been intercepted by the French fleet under Admiral Suffren, and on the 15th of February a long but indecisive battle was fought. By the 26th of March Boyd was at Trincomalee, where the garrison had been strengthened ; as his ship had already departed he set out immediately in a small vessel which he chartered, but had the misfortune on the way to fall into the hands of Suffren, who on the 12th of April again engaged the Britlsh fleet in the Bay. Both sides suffered severely, the British having 567 casualties, and then the French withdrew.

The British however received little assistance from the King ; they were in such difficulties about provisions that their Sepoys were kept from deserting with great trouble. Nevertheless their vessels were hovering about the neighbourhood of Manar and making the western road dangerous. The Company therefore anticipating a landing at Chilaw, where the fort had been allowed to fall into ruins, sent a garrison there and arrranged beacon lights all along the coast as far as Colombo, to give notice of the approach of the enemy.

At Colombo itself elaborate additions to the fortifications, which were greatly dilapidated in parts, were commenced under the supervision of an ex-surveyor named Rymers, but these, it was suggested, were merely a pretext for robbing the Company. The suggestion was not by any means improbable ; at any rate a singularly lax condition of discipline prevailed among the military forces. The forts at both Negumbo and Puttalam were in a ruinous condition ; the garrison, consisting chiefly of Tupasses and Malays, were permitted to quarter themselves among the neighbouring villagers ; and the main portion of the Puttalam fort was found occupied by a French woman and her daughter.

On the 27th of August Suffren, who had been refitting at Galle and Batticaloa, appeared unexpectedly before Trincomalee and proceeded to land men and raise batteries. In three days the fort surrendered, and the garrison was allowed to return to Madras.

This did not improve their condition much, for Suffren with his head quarters at Trincomalee, was able to blockade Madras till the inhabitants suffered from all the horrors of famine. The British plans had completely miscarried, and it was fortunate for the Hollanders that it was so. The Company's servants were not to be trusted, and Raket, the Commandeur at Jaffnapatnam, was in correspondence with the enemy; indeed the terms of surrender were all ready in his hands, and only the failure of the British to arrive saved the place for the Hollanders for a few years longer. Trincomalee was finally restored to the Company in 1784, along with the rest of its dismantled factories in India.

On the 5th of February 1785 Falck died at his country residence at Malwatta near Nagalagama after a short illness, and two days later Wilhelm Jacob van der Graaf, an officer of great ability who at the time was Commandeur of Galle, took charge of the administration. The following month the aged Abayasinha of Galle was appointed Maha Mudaliyar; he had as Mudaliyar of the Galle Guard come into prominence during the troublous times of Schreuder, who had gratefully recorded his obligations to him on a plate of gold. Another medal and chain were now presented to him, and till his death in 1794 he continued to exercise a great influence on the Governor.

Through this Maha Mudaliyar's hands passed all the correspondence with the Ministers, for the recent trouble with the British had created a difficult situation. The Court successfully insisted on the humiliating ceremonies which had been abolished in 1766 being resumed by the Company's ambasadors, and pressed for the restoration of the western coast. The latter the Company would not surrender, and the relations between the parties grew more and more strained.

The attitude of the Nawab in respect of the Pearl Fishery increased the difficulties of the Governor; an abortive treaty was entered into with his agent in 1785 but was repudiated by the Nawab. The consequence of this trouble was that no fishery had been held since 1768. Fortunately the Governor of Madras, Sir Archibald Campbell, was a personal friend of van der Graaf, and exerted his influence with the Nawab with such good effect that on the 7th of July 1788 a Treaty was entered into at Colombo between the Governor and the Nawab's Agent James Buchanan, by which the Company ceded to the Nawab half the Tutucorin fishery and the right to thirty six boats in the Ceylon Fishery. Moreover his representative at the Fishery was allowed to hoist his own flag and to maintain a separate military guard, so long as he complied with the fishery regulations of the Company. The concessions were very heavy, but the Company was glad to arrive at some settlement of the harassing dispute.

In the meantime the situation in Europe had changed in a remarakble fashion. On the 15th of April 1788 a Treaty had been entered into at The Hague by which the British undertook to assist the Settlements belonging to the United Provinces in case of hostilities with France, and in September 1789 Lord Cornwallis wrote from Fort William to assure van der Graaf of his anxiety effectively to carry out this promise. The friendly feeling thus brought about was made use of by van der Graaf to obtain rice from the British settlements for the relief of Ceylon, which again was suffering from a shortage. The following year Lord Cornwallis in turn appealed to the Governor for assistance against Tippu Sultan who had attacked the Travancore Raja, an ally of the British, and also begged him to keep a careful eye on the proceedings of the French.

Negotiations had been proceeding between these last and the King, who had applied to them for protection against the Company. The people of the Chilaw District, which was being administered from Colombo, were restless; they insisted on nominating their own chief, and van der Graaf had been obliged to acquiesce, for it was found that opposition only led to rioting and to the inhabitants fleeing to the King. There were serious outbreaks in the Colombo Disawani, and even the Giruwayas were in a state of turmoil.

It was realised that the Sinhalese in the Company's territory still had the utmost respect for the orders of the King, and that the presence of his armed forces was regarded with terror. The Lascarins who were sent to guard the salt pans in the west were found to have fraternised with the King's men and to have sold their ammunition to the latter. The Company was harassed by repeated outbreaks of small-pox which caused much loss of life; the King's country fortunately was saved from infection by the great forests which guarded its frontiers. There was a lack of rice, and the demand for fresh meat to feed the increased military forces was so great, that the price of the animals which were brought from the Munesseram District was nearly doubled.

At last the King closed his *Kadawatu*, and it was feared that hostilities could not be avoided much longer. Van der Graaf appears to have entered into a treasonable correspondence with Pilima Talauwa, son of Kirti Sri Raja Sinha's Adigar, who was now a Disawa. The details are obscure, but the Governor seems to have been persuaded that he could take possession of Sabaragamuwa, and in June 1791 Colonel de Meuron with his regiment of Swiss mercenaries, which was in the service of the Company, supported by a large body of Hollanders, Malays, and Lascarins, advanced into the Disawani. Pilima Talauwa was expected to join him, but not a soul was to be seen in the country, and not a morsel of food could be found. De Meuron, who had pushed on to Kendangomuwa, found himself cut off in the midst of a morass, exposed for three days to the torrential rains for which the District is well known. There was nothing to be done but to beat an immediate retreat to Sitawaka, at the same time sending word to van der Graaf, who was awaiting developments at Hanwella, to send him assistance; only an accident, it was said, saved his force from destruction.

CHAPTER X

The Council at Batavia, whose anxieties with regard to the finances of the Company had been greatly increased by the intrusion of Danish and American vessels within Eastern waters, was distracted at the threatening condition of affairs ; it was also worried over its relations with the Raja of Cochin, who was an ally of the British ; accordingly in 1792 it sent definite instructions that whatever happened war with the King was to be avoided. The position was humiliating, when fortunately the King of his own accord opened his *Kadawatu.* The season for peeling cinnamon was close at hand, but van der Graaf was unwilling to send the usual embassy to obtain permission. The Ministers when approached on the subject, made it clear that permission would not be granted without the yearly embassy, and for 1793 the Company had to content itself with the produce of its own territory.

This was the less difficult owing to the gratifying results which had attended its attempts to cultivate cinnamon. The natives had taken kindly to the work, and the number of gardens planted for the Company increased so rapidly, that very serious difficulty was encountered in keeping them free from weeds. Abayasinha thereupon suggested that the Chalias should be placed in charge of allotments, from the produce of which they could pay their duty : this plan was adopted by the Council in 1791, and was soon a brilliant success. Andris Mendis and Dines de Zoysa, Mudaliyar and Maha Vidane respectively of the Mahabadda, were found most helpful, and received warm commendations from the Governor. Everiyawatta was planted by Mendis and Kadirana by de Zoysa, and there was good reason to expect that very soon the Company would be independent ot the supply from the King's dominions.

Others besides the members of the caste interested themselves in the work; for instance the Second Maha Mudaliyar, Wijayasekara Abayaratna, nephew of Lienderan de Saram, made a large plantation at Dematagoda, and also planted pepper and coffee in the important Vidaneships of Kelaniya and Ambatale. The Company showed its gratitude to all these by presenting them with gold chains and medals.

The Sinhalese had the instinct natural to men whose knowledge did not extend much beyond their villages; their craving for such tokens of honour was inordinate, even though the Fountain of Honour was no longer a semi-divine King, but a merchant on a monthly salary and allowances. A gold *Sannas* was a distinction rarely bestowed even among those of the Royal Blood, and something of its glamour attached itself to the Medal, which had the further attraction that it could be worn about the person. The Company very well understood how to turn to its own advantage this amiable weakness, which cost it very little. It is curious to think that in spite of the spread of Western ideas and manners, this craving still maintains so firm a hold, that instances are not unknown of private individuals presenting such marks of their esteem to their friends, who even make a display of them at public functions.

A similar reward had been given by Falck to Bandaranayaka, Mudaliyar of the Siyane Korale, whose great grandfather Mohotti Appuhami had been specially recommended by van Goens in 1663 to the consideration of his successor. Bandaranayaka planted Siyambalape, and came into prominence again during the recent troubles with the Court; and van der Graaf conferred on him, at the same time as on Abayaratna, a second Medal and the title of Maha Mudaliyar.

Cultivation was encouraged in the South by inserting in the appointments of Mudaliyars a condition that they must plant a specified acreage within a stated time. So great was the enthusiasm displayed over cinnamon that in Colombo the supply of labour for the cultivation of rice was affected adversely. An embankment however was raised to protect a large tract of fields at Grandpass, the cost of the work being charged to the owners who were benefited by it. A dam from Ambatale to Panadura was proposed with a view to increasing the food resources of Colombo. Another dam at Biagama and a Canal in the Pasdum Korale were suggested in 1742 by Governor Overbeek, who took much interest in rice cultivation.

The question of draining the important village of Diviture had been raised by Pielat, but the Batavian authorities were unwilling to incur the expense; they declared however that if the inhabitants would undertake the task at their own cost, the Company would at some future date give them such recognition as they deserved. In spite of this discouraging attitude some progress had been made with the work, and a new scheme was under consideration to drain that village and Gangaboda Pattu by giving the Gin Ganga a fresh outlet near Baddegama into the Hikkaduwa Lake. An attempt was made to reclaim the large tract of lowlying and marshy land, estimated at a thousand *amunams*, which lay between Polatu Oya and Matara. With this object in view Canals were opened and dams erected at great expense, but the difficulties encountered at Mutu Raja Wela again presented themselves, and it was found not to be possible to exclude the salt.

The Giruwayas had been greatly benefited by leading down into its rich fields the waters of the Nilwala Ganga, and this served also to protect the lower reaches of the river from those disastrous floods which are the feature of tropical rivers. Burnand had opened a canal at Batticaloa, and the work was so successful that the paddy revenue of the district increased four-fold, and in addition a large extent of coconut land was rendered available for cultivation; but the rest of the east was badly neglected, for the Company could never bring itself to spend the money which was required for irrigation.

A report was prepared in 1793 on Maha Sen's great tank of Gantalawa, which even in its neglected state could irrigate three thousand *parrahs*, though the supply of water was uncertain. Tampalakamam had been occupied in 1766 and contained a fairly large Tamil population, who regarded the tank with religious awe. The district itself was greatly neglected, and the Company's half-hearted attempts to set matters right were interrupted by the occupation of the neighbourhood first by the British and then by the French. Some armed Kaffirs who had escaped from the latter for a long time pillaged and murdered through the District, and whole villages were abandoned at the approach of these reputed black cannibals. Disease was rife; smallpox raged from time to time; and the only remedy was to flee from the infected villages, for there was no medical provision. The headmen who had helped to bring the District under the Company, were left to oppress the people without control; they levied heavy fines till no one ventured to display any signs of wealth, and while they exacted compulsory labour from the villager without any reference to the needs of his cultivation, they gave little help in organising that combined effort which was essential in dealing with tracts of field in the forest. The villager who as a rule was loaded with debt, was not secure even in the tenure of his lands; for the headmen would take them from one and give them to another according to their own fancy.

The rich lands of the Karachchi had been the subject of abortive schemes since the time of Overbeek, while van Goens himself had drawn attention to Kattu karai, Giant's Tank. Nothing was done till Falck made an attempt to have the Tank repaired by the Tamils of Jaffna who were subject to the Uliyam; they however soon ran away and the work was abandoned. Van der Graaf had a fresh survey made, and proposed to develop the tank lands by a private Company, but on instructions received from Batavia in 1792 this scheme too was abandoned, and twenty years later a score of villages still occupied the bed of the tank.

The natural line of water communication which was available on the western coast was blocked for several miles between Kaymel and Maravila, and in consequence goods had to be transhipped by coolies at great expense. In the case of the Company this was done free of charge by the Paduwo as their Rajakariya. There was a proposal in 1790 to remove the obstruction, but owing to the troubles with the King the matter was dropped.

Chilaw itself was in a satisfactory condition. The rice fields were flourishing; valuable gardens of pepper, coffee, and coconut had been opened; teak plantations were made in various parts; while the manioc, introduced by Van der Graaf through the help of a Catholic Priest, added greatly to the food supply of the inhabitants.

In 1778 the Company ceased to buy arecanut direct from the producers; anyone was now at liberty to purchase from them provided he sold it again to the Company at a price which was fixed from time to time. The Company in turn sold the article at a profit of nearly 200 per cent, and during van der Graaf's term of office the net revenue from areca alone averaged 79000 florins a year. The King's subjects too were reaping the advantage of higher prices from the Coast merchants, and van der Graaf proposed to get that traffic once again under the Company's control. As for the elephants, in view of the great expenditure involved of labour which could be more advantageously employed in other ways, he considered the profits of the hunt to be more imaginary than real. Moreover the troubles with the British had interfered seriously with their capture in the North. His idea was to purchase them from private captors in the Wanni and Batticaloa and to sell them outside, and a contract based on this scheme was entered into with Vaitilingam Chetty, the wealthy renter of Jaffna who for several years farmed the Chank fishery. The Matara Hunt, he thought, should be limited to the object of keeping down the herds when they began to prove a nuisance to the inhabitants. The publication of Buffon's Natural History led to much interesting correspondence with experienced natives in the South regarding the habits and life history of the animal. A detailed report of the tricks performed in 1786 by a trained tusker at the King's Palace for the diversion of the Company's Ambassadors, has been preserved.

Since 1758 the paddy duty had been collected on account of the Company direct, but it was found that this led to much loss in consequence of the dishonesty of the Commissioners, who had to appraise the crops. Van der Graaf therefore began once again to farm out the tax.

Much interest was taken in growing and manufacturing cotton, and in 1793 a certain John Vervyk, who claimed to have experience of the work in South India, proposed a scheme for its development at Jaffna. He demanded for himself ten per cent of the profits, and a free hand in dealing with the labour force whenever he was obliged "to act in earnest with them for bad conduct." Weavers were brought and settled at Chilaw, Colombo and Matara, and there was a large amount of cloth made at Batticaloa, Manar and Puttalam, but the bulk of the cotton had to be obtained from the Seven Korales and Nuwara Kalawaya. A sugar plantation was opened at Kalutara, and Colonel de Meuron made both sugar and rum between Colombo and Galkissa.

Although van der Graaf reduced the number of the mercenary regiments to two, yet the increased military expenditure continued to be a serious handicap to progress. The Directors pressed for revenue from all conceivable sources, but the expenses always exceeded the income obtained locally, and the deficit had to be made good from the profits of the cinnamon trade in Europe, which were earmarked for dividends.

The unreliability of the Civil Service aggravated the situation; the evils so frequent in a Colony abounded under the Hollanders, and Ceylon was treated as a convenient spot where blockheads, libertines, and bankrupts, who had influence with the Directorate, could easily be dumped. According to ancient Sinhalese custom a headman on appointment paid a *bulat surulla* to the Mudaliyar whose influence had secured him the distinction. This practice had grown into scandalous proportions, but the Governors and Disawas who in their turn expected and received from the Mudaliyars tokens of gratitude similar in nature but proportionate to their own exalted stations, found it convenient to wink at the abuse. Fortunately the condition of things had not yet been aggravated by depriving the headmen of their *badawedili*.

Falck and after him his successor tried hard to cope with the scandal, but the weight of the entire public service was cast into the scale against them. Both these able Governors did much to improve the finances by insisting on probity in all Departments, by introducing a reasonable amount of order in the administration, by suppressing extravagance, and simplifying the collection of revenue. Their efforts met with a fair share of success, and van der Graaf was able to relieve the strain caused by the military expenditure; it was asserted that he increased the local revenue by one half.

Taking everything into consideration, the condition of the Sinhalese within the Settlements had improved since the expulsion of the Portuguese. The number of the Company's subjects had increased, but was still almost beyond doubt under half a million. The poverty of the villager was still very great; money was scarce, and nearly all the trade was in the hands of the Burghers. The Company no doubt was an exacting task-master, but it assured the infinite blessing of peace. The terrible stories of Portuguese times were now a memory of the past, and the villager had the certainty that some portion at least of his labour would enure to his own benefit. He had a fair measure of personal security, and a reasonable likelihood of even-handed justice. His children had the chance of acquiring some slight knowledge of letters, and no one could drive him away arbitrarily from his tenement. This was a great deal gained.

In the case of the upper classes the effect had been greater. Their social manners and customs were changing, but not with the same rapidity as under the Portuguese. Intermarriage which was so common in the time of the latter, was no longer in favour; and it is doubtful if a dozen Sinhalese of position took wives from among the Hollanders. Since the beginning of the century intermarriage was officially discouraged, for it was thought that the two generations which had come into existence since the occupation of Galle in 1640, had produced enough daughters with European fathers, to satisfy the requirements of the Hollanders. No respectable Sinhalese, except perhaps the one or two who had been to Europe, wore European costume; indeed in 1741 two high-born maiden ladies disinherited the young man who was their next of kin on the ground that he had adopted European clothes and manners. The Maha Mudaliyar still appeared bare-footed before the Governor, and never presumed to sit down in his presence.

Substantial houses were taking the place of the mud walls of their grandfathers, and this was especially the case in towns like Colombo and Matara. Good furniture made of calamander and ebony was to be seen in these houses, though in limited quantities; good porcelain and excellent Venetian glass of these times still attract the collector to the lumber rooms of their descendants. The jewels worn by ladies, which had degenerated under the Portuguese, were now replaced by remarkably skilful copies of European models, set with diamonds and emeralds. A betel box of ivory or tortoise-shell inlaid with gold was as necessary to a great lady as a silver tea-service is today.

Rice fields still formed the most important kind of landed property; coconut plantations however were increasing rapidly in number, though the size of individual lands was not great; a hundred acres would have been an unusually large plantation. Since 1780 the great demand for arrack had led to a large increase in the number of distilleries along the coast and their owners made much money. The price of nuts rose as high as 12 rix dollars a thousand by 1796, though the heavy cost of transport to Colombo affected the profits.

The Hollander loved his food and his wife cooked it well, and the wealthier Sinhalese followed him in this, though at a great distance. We read of a Sinhalese funeral assembly, when according to "the Colombo fashion", the mourners were served with "wine, beer, bacon, cheese, butter, bread, gin, brandy, other kinds of wine, and sweetmeats." Spoons and forks of silver were to be seen at their tables, and their rooms were lit not only by the tall brass lamps which are still in use, but also by globes of glass suspended from the roof, and containing a wick floating in coconut oil. Slaves were largely employed as domestics, though perhaps not to the same extent as among the European officials; twenty-one of them were mentioned by name in the Will of Abayasinha.

At marriages and funerals which were conducted according to Christian rites, the customs of the Hollanders were generally followed, and the *koronchi* or crowning of the bride on her return from the Church to the parents' house, which is still in use, is a survival from these times. Among non-Christians, however, the old Sinhalese marriage ceremonies continued; the bride and the bridegroom were placed on the white-covered *Magul Poruwa*, which was sprinkled with rice, and after the groom had presented the bride with a gold chain and a cloth, their thumbs were tied together with a thread, and water or milk poured over them. As a rule rings also were exchanged between them.

Jaffna alone had not advanced on the wave of prosperity, though even at this time it had the reputation of being the Province were Officials made the largest and most rapid fortunes; in spite of the ceaseless industry of its people, it was said to be getting poorer, and more lands were sold there in satisfaction of debts than in any other part of the country.

Probably less than half a million souls formed that remnant of the Sinhalese which still boasted a nominal independence under its Dravidian Monarch. Little could be said of it except that it still existed, for the struggle of the East against the intrusion of the West, so long and so tenaciously maintained, was nearly over. Laws and customs had not altered since Kotte was abandoned and Alagiyawanna sang the glories of the Sitawaka of Raja Sinha. Stagnation, intellectual, material, and moral, oppressed it like a nightmare; life was a long drudgery, a weary struggle for food and a little clothing, relieved only by the excitement of a visit to the temple, with its rich-toned and sometimes beautiful frescoes. The comforts and refinements of life were unknown; wealth, as it was found along the sea coast, was not heard of. Trade was of the scantiest, and the little which existed was monopolised by the men in power; means of communication were of the most primitive; manufactures hardly existed, and the amount of coin in circulation was strictly limited; the money revenue of the King was probably less than that of some of the Mudaliyars in the service of the Company.

Public works were nearly unknown, though much was done for religious edifices. The Sinhalese man had little to hope for, nothing to aspire to; he was discouraged from cultivating more than was needed to supply the bare necessities of life; he was full of gratitude if that life was safe and his plantation remained unplundered; he was exultant if he raised a little coin by selling his arecanuts. Beyond that he had no outlook. It is a depressing picture, but the inheritance of a great past preserved in him the seed of future possibilities.

There was one matter which militated against the general prosperity of the Settlements, and that was the question of exchange. From the beginning a variety of coins had been accepted as currency by the Company. Not only the Sinhalese silver *ridi* or *laryn,* the copper *massas* and gold *fanams,* together with the various Portuguese issues of Goa and Colombo, but even Persian, German, and Spanish coins were in circulation. The most popular were the thin copper duits which were coined by the various provinces of the Netherlands, and imported into the country in large quantities, along with a small proportion of silver stivers, schellings, florins and ducatoons. Gold pagodas were coined at the Tutucorin mint which was under the supervision of Colombo, and the various other pagodas of South India were accepted according to their metal value compared with the ducatoon. The local copper coinage consisted of the thick stivers, thirty of which weighed a pound, which were minted at a great profit in the island, along with the two-stiver pieces and fractions of the stiver. A few silver rupees also were issued by Falck and van der Graaf.

Goods required for the Settlements were imported mainly from Holland and Batavia in the vessels of the Company, and their cost was met by bills on those countries, on which the Company made a profit. The imports from India were balanced in part by exports from Ceylon, but there remained an excess which had to be paid for in gold and silver.

The quantity of the precious metals in the country was extremely small, and in view of the financial embarrassments subsequent to 1780, van der Graaf conceived the idea of issuing a paper currency in the form of notes called Kredit Brieven, payable to the bearer in copper at a fixed rate. All payments from the Treasury were made in these notes or in copper, and in a short time the supply of silver and gold coin available for export to India was exhausted. The Governor therefore proceeded to sell these coins by public auction, and in ten years a ducatoon which under the Company's regulations was worth only eighty stivers, was sold for a hundred. At the same time in the case of remittances to Holland the Treasury insisted that at least half the sum should be tendered in silver.

This exchange was carried on at the original rate, and the officials who remitted their salaries to the mother country, shared in the profit; whereas the price of grain, cotton, and similar necessaries imported from India rose with rapidity and the local consumer suffered heavily. It was the value of the ducatoon which had originally fixed the rate of exchange, but now the copper coin became the real standard, and exchange was adjusted in accordance with the actual value of the copper contained in the stiver. This copper was much depreciated, and in 1787 the coins were struck from the old brass guns, which were melted down for the purpose, thereby adding to the complexity of the situation.

Disturbing rumours began to reach Ceylon towards the end of 1793 that France had declared war on Holland and England, and with a heavy heart van der Graaf once again turned to those military questions which were so repugnant to the Company. The available forces consisted of 4000 infantry including the de Meuron and Wurtemberg regiments of mercenaries, with 700 Artillery. There were also two small bodies of well trained Lascarins in charge of the Maha Mudaliyar at Colombo and the Atapattu Mudaliyar at Galle respectively, as well as some Moors at Batticaloa. Orders were given to have the forts in readiness against possible hostilities, and Trincomalee was placed at the disposal of the British war-ships. Karikal and Pondicherri were soon occupied by British troops, but French frigates were cruising about the Indian waters; and van der Graaf while sending 800 men to assist in defending the Indian coast had to appeal to Fort St. George for effective protection by sea.

In the meantime he had received his appointment as Director General at Batavia, and on the

10th of January 1794 his father-in-law, van Angelbeek, arrived from the Choromandel Coast to succeed him in office. Van der Graaf sailed away in August, having four months before in company with van Angelbeek, accompanied the body of his trusted Maha Mudaliyar to the grave. Abayasinha died at the age of seventy five years, and was buried with all the honours usually accorded to his high office; sixteen of the Company's Sergeants carried his coffin to the grave, over which a company of soldiers fired three vollies of musketry. On the following day Abayaratna, the second Maha Mudaliyar, was appointed in his place.

Hardly had van der Graaf left the country when unpleasantness arose with the British. The latter had long regarded with envious eyes the rich trade in the cotton goods of South India which the Hollanders enjoyed, and now made a bold bid to obtain some portion of this trade for themselves. Thereupon in August the Hollanders seized a British vessel with a cargo of piece goods, claiming a monopoly in the trade under a series of treaties dating from 1690, and by prescriptive right. They maintained that their right was recognised even in the treaty which Buchanan had signed on behalf of the Nawab, and that the treaty was brought about by the active interference of Governor Campbell himself. Therefore they insisted that all vessels trading on that coast must obtain their passport, and were also liable to be searched,

Lord Hobart who was at Madras refused to acknowledge this claim. The Nayaker, he argued, could not bind his successors in this fashion; even if he could, the Nawab who had succeeded him by right of conquest, was not only not bound by his acts, but was himself barred by prior treaties from entering into any agreement with a European power without the consent of the British; and the British, he said, declined to ratify Buchanan's treaty. After much wrangling, in June 1795 van Angelbeek agreed to Lord Hobart's proposal to refer the matter to Europe.

In the meanwhile in December 1794 of the French had entered the Netherlands; the Hereditary Stadtholder fled to England for safety, and a new Batavian Republic was established over the United Provinces, in alliance with France. Barely had the last dispatch with reference to the Indian dispute left Colombo, when a fresh letter arrived from Hobart. This accompanied one from the late Stadtholder, dated Kew, 7th of February 1795, in which he requested Van Angelbeek to admit his Britannic Majesty's men and ships within the Settlements in his charge, and to treat them as allies coming to protect the Settlements from the French.

On the strength of this letter Hobart claimed the immediate possession of all the Settlements, with an assurance that they would be restored when the independence of the States was re-established by a general Peace. He promised to maintain the existing laws and customs, to impose no fresh taxes, and to leave the internal trade entirely free; all officers would continue to serve till the pleasure of the British King was known, and the men would be taken over on the existing terms. He concluded by stating that a military force had already started for Trincomalee in case of resistance being offered to the proposed occupation.

The Council replied on the 27th of July that the Stadtholder had said nothing about handing over the Settlements to the British; but it was ready to give all assistance to their vessels and to receive garrisons at Colombo and Trincomalee, provided the Madras authorities would defray the expenses till such time as matters could be adjusted in Europe.

Hobart's messenger, Major Agnew, and two Hollanders, started at once with this reply for Trincomalee, where the British fleet under Commodore Rainer with a small army under Colonel Stuart had already arrived. On the 2nd of August communications were opened with Major Fornbauer, who was in command of the forts, when Agnew arrived with the Governor's reply. The British were willing to accept the terms offered but Fornbauer refused to agree, on the ground that the letter was signed not by the members of the Council but by Van Angelbeek alone.

Stuart thereupon landed his men at a point two miles from the Fort, losing in the process a frigate which struck on a sunken rock. The small garrison made a good defence ; the Malays, employing their Gurkha-like tactics, succeeded in entering one of the British batteries, killing the artillery men, and spiking the guns. The fire from the walls caused some loss of life, but at the end of three weeks a breach was effected, and Fornbauer, one of the few brave officers the Company possessed, was forced to surrender. According to the terms of the capitulation, which was signed on the 26th of August, the garrison was allowed the honours of war. Five days later Fort Ostenberg also fell, and British troops were sent to occupy Batticaloa.

The Court was watching events with much satisfaction, and kept the British well supplied with provisions. Robert Andrews, a Senior Merchant in their Company's service, had accompained the expedition to Ceylon, where he was destined to leave behind an evil name. On the 15th of September he started from Trincomalee with a letter from Lord Hobart to the King, by whom he was received in audience on the 29th, with the same ceremonial as had been followed in the case of Pybus.

Pilima Talauwa and Erawwawala, the Adigars, and the Council of Ministers showed themselves capable men of business. Andrews' first request was for a site belonging to the King, where his Company could erect a fort and build a factory; it was imperative, he insisted, that this should be a spot to which the Hollanders could have no title. The Ministers in return shrewdly demanded a guarantee that nothing taken from the Hollanders would at any time be returned to them. Andrews was unable to comply with this demand, but suggested that the inland districts taken by force from the King might be returned to him instead. He also claimed the same trade monopoly as the Hollanders enjoyed; but the Ministers, while agreeing to give preference to the British, reserved to themselves the right to sell to any other nation which was willing to pay a higher price.

Andrews tried to obtain a copy of the arrangements existing with the Hollanders, but was curtly refused. The preliminaries of a Treaty were signed on the 12th of October and he returned to Trincomalee with Dumbara Rala, a son of the conqueror of Hanwella, and another who were authorised to continue negotiations at Madras.

Meanwhile a British force had landed at Point Pedro, and being joined by fresh men from Nagapatnam, advanced on Jaffnapatnam. On the 28th of September Stuart sent to the garrison, which had been reduced to a few Sepoys and some invalid officers, a summons to surrender; resistance was out of the question, and the fine fort, on which so much money and labour had been spent, yielded without firing a shot.

On the 12th of November Dumbara Rala arrived by land at Jaffna, from where the Sinhalese Mission consisting of over a hundred souls, took ship for the Continent. The frankness of Lord Hobart, who plainly stated that the question of the entire exclusion of the Hollanders could be decided only in Europe, caused bitter disappointment to the Sinhalese, but after much wrangling a Treaty was signed on Friday the 12th of February 1796. This provided among other matters, for the site of a factory, preferential trade, the restoration to the King of all territory occupied by force, with some salt pans and a limited right of foreign trade, as well as for the protection of the Buddhist religion. This Treaty had to be ratified by the King within a fixed period, but by the time Dumbara Rala returned to Court, a very great change had taken place.

With the fall of Trincomalee, the Council had realised that hostilities could not be avoided any longer and active preparations were made to defend Colombo. The artillery was rearranged so as to command all points from which danger was expected, fresh batteries were raised, the surrounding country was cleared of the trees and houses which might impede the action of the guns, and the Moors were organised into three companies of coolies. The tanks within the Fort were filled with drinking water, and all private wells were cleaned out and put into order. A large quantity of live stock was collected and stores of dried fish, rice and arrack laid in, while people from outside who sought refuge within the walls were ordered to bring with them provisions sufficient for six months. The cinnamon collected at the various outstations was brought to the stores at Colombo, though much had to be abandoned at Galle for lack of means of transport.

About this time two vessels arrived from Batavia with official information of the Treaty which had been entered into between Holland and France, whereupon all effective troops were ordered back to Colombo from Jaffna, the Wanni and Manar. A few days after the surrender of Jaffna, Agnew arrived at Colombo with another letter from Hobart, in which he informed van Angelbeek that Count de Meuron, the proprietor of the regiment which bore his name, had transferred its services to the British by an agreement entered into on the 30th of March, and demanded that the men should be handed over to him.

Agnew was lodged within the fort and was hospitably entertained by van Angelbeek with whom he dined every day; he thus had the opportunity of observing from the Governor's balcony all the preparations which were made to resist the enemy. In spite of a defiant reply which van Angelbeek promptly despatched to Hobart, his attitude towards the regiment was noteworthy. A large number of the men were French or Hollanders and had no desire to take service under the British, but the Governor, it was said, urged them to go. Vessels for their transport were lacking, and the sloops of the Company were placed at their disposal for a small consideration, while the sick who could not travel were kept in the Company's hospital and looked after as if they were still in its service.

On the departure of this regiment the Council decided to abandon Galle, and the artillery and ammunition were removed to Colombo. British vessels were cruising about the coast, and even landing men to obtain provisions; the shore batteries were accordingly manned at night, but strict instructions were given that no gun was to be fired without the express orders of the Governor. The vessels passed and repassed, approaching Colombo quite close at night, but the order to fire never came. A French vessel commanded by a Hollander entered the harbour, and the commander offered to capture the British vessels if he were furnished with some artillery men for the guns, but this offer was not entertained.

In January 1796 Colonel Stuart's army was collected at Rameswaram, and on the 10th started from there in open boats. Every evening the men landed for rest, and no opposition was encountered. The Company's officers in charge of Kalpitiya and Chilaw retreated in haste to Colombo, and a military force which was sent as far as Kaymel followed their example. Not a soldier was seen within the square fort of Negombo, which had been built with the special object of protecting the chief cinnamon district of the Island. The British occupied the place, where they were joined by Wikramasinha Mudaliyar, who was able to keep them supplied with provisions.

The delightful fertility and healthfulness of the country charmed the newcomers; beautiful coconut groves and rich fields lay on every side, fish and foodstuffs were abundant, the population was large and industrious, and trading vessels frequented the small harbour. A fairly good road, probably the best the Company had formed in Ceylon, connected the town with Colombo. No attempt was made to bar the advance of the army, and Stuart was allowed to reach the Kelani Ganga without opposition.

Dry rot had set in among the Hollanders. That retribution which so surely a waits the commercial race which has no ideal beyond the exploitation of the country of another for its own aggrandisement, had fallen upon the men. The one aim of the Hollander was the speedy acquisition of wealth. The indomitable courage which once defied the might of Philip of Spain, had dissolved in the ardent heat of a tropical sun. If Captain Robert Percival, who arrived in Ceylon in this very year, is to be believed, the Hollander began his day with gin and tobacco, and he ended it with tobacco and gin. In the interval he fed grossly, lounged about, indulged in the essential siesta, and transacted a little business. The women folk, who spent most of their time chewing betel and gossiping in Portuguese with their slaves, did not come up to the somewhat exacting standard of the fastidious Captain.

In spite of the departure of the de Meuron Regiment, over 2500 Europeans, Malays, Moors, and Sepoys were still available to defend Colombo. There were in addition five hundred fierce Chalias trained to work among forests, and the Lascarins. So strong a force fighting behind walls, could well defy an invading army for a great length of time. It was expected that the passage of the Kelani Ganga would be stoutly defended by the batteries which commanded it on the Colombo side. The Company's troops occupied the river bank from Pas Betal, the scene of so many bloody fights between Sinhalese and Portuguese, as far as Nagalagama. Stuart spent two days in making his preparations, till on the 9th of February the bulk of the defending force withdrew towards Mutwal, and at 5 p. m. the British began to cross. A few shots were fired at them from the nearest battery, and then the men threw the guns into the water, and disappeared. The British hurried across on bamboo rafts without further hindrance, and occupied a strong position where they could be supported by their vessels from the sea. It was known that the King's forces too were approaching Colombo from the East so as to assist them. Within the fort everything was in confusion, discipline had ceased to exist, the officers were not anxious to expose themselves to the enemy's bullets, and the men had lost their *morale.* By degrees the various detachments in the field retired till they assembled at Korteboom, backed by the forest which then existed in the neighbourhood. An enemy frigate approached the harbour whereupon some of the batteries opened fire, but the officers in command were immediately placed under arrest for doing so without the Governor's orders.

On the 12th of February at 3 A. M. a body of Malays, whose tactics and sharp krises were alike a matter of apprehension to the British, set out from Colombo. They were joined by a number of deserters from the de Meuron regiment, as well as a gallant Frenchman, Colonel Raymond, of the late Luxemburg Regiment. It was declared that some of the Hollanders accompanied the Malays, but not further than the outer wall. The attempt to surprise the enemy which followed was not attended with much success and the Malays were driven back, Raymond himself being mortally wounded. The British now advanced to Korteboom, whereupon Kayman's Gate was closed and all the military retired within the Castle, leaving behind a few Malays in charge.

On the 13th the British approached the Gate and encamped near the ruins of a Portuguese battery. The men who had fought in 1656 within that battery for the possession of this beautiful Island had indeed been cast in a different mould from those who, skulking behind the walls of Colombo, still claimed that coveted prize. Van Angelbeek now opened secret negociations. No further opposition was offered, and the only excitement was that caused by a couple of buffaloes straying within the British lines; for the alarm was given and the guards firing wildly had the misfortune to kill two of their own men.

At one P. M. on the 14th Major Agnew appeared at Kayman's Gate and van Angelbeek's carriage conveyed him to the Castle, where he was received by the Council: after a long interview he returned to the camp in the evening. There were wild rumours of an immediate suspension of hostilities, and the troops were mutinous, for they feared that they were going to be betrayed. Early in the morning of the 16th firing, all directed at the Governor's house, broke out from various parts of the Fort, but in a short time the announcement was made that hostilities were ended. At 10 o'clock in the morning the Company's possessions in the Island were surrendered to the British, and its military forces, with undamaged limbs and uncrumpled tunics, marched out of the Castle.

It was believed both at the time and also after van Angelbeek's death, that he had sold himself to the British. That might well be the case; at any rate he burnt less powder in defence of Colombo than Jan Schreuder had fired in honour of one letter to the Sinhalese King.

THE END

INDEX

Abayaratna, Maha Mudaliyar. 148, 160 (Johannes de Saram, Wijayasekera, b. 1754, d. 17th Nov. 1809)
Abayasinha, Maha Mudaliyar. 143, 147, 160 (Nicholas Dias, Amarasekara, b. 8th May 1719, d. 10th May 1794)
Accommodessan, see Badawedili
Adam, 31
Adam's Peak, see Samanala
Adigar, 31, 56, 68, 103, 104, 109, 111, 114, 162, 163
Administrateur, Hoofd, 72
Administration, see Company
Adukku, 129
Agnew, Major, 162-168
Agoa de Lopo, 33
Agriculture, see Rice, Pepper, Canal, Tank, etc.
Alagiyawanna, 157
Aldear, 108
Allauwa, 26
Almeyda, Lourenco de, 3
Alphandigo, 82
Alut Kuru Korale, 129
Alvis, Paulo Mudlr. 85
Alwis, see Samarasinha
Ambanwela Rala, 22, 24
Ambatale, 148, 149
America, 140, 147
Ampitiya, 103, 136
Amsterdam, 90
Amu, 126
Amunam, see Areca
Andi 70
Andrews, Robert, 162, 163
Angelbeek, J. G. Van, 114, 119, 162-169
Anguruwatota, 1
Ant, 85
Anuradhapura, 28
Appuhami, 89, 130
Arachchi. 128
Arandora, 14, 17, 26
Arcot, 64
Areca 13, 25, 40, 50, 52, 54, 57, 63 77, 86, 99, 103, 120, 122, 151
Aripo, 22, 55
Arrack, 20, 39, 60, 82, 86, 87, 124, 128, 155
Arrakan, 43, 44
Arrow, 115
Artillery, 21, 104, 105, 114, 162
Asadrisa, Jatakaya, 136
Aswala Rala, 31
Asylum, see Leprosy
Astronomy, 138
Atakalan Korale, 138
Atchin, 86
Attapattu, 76, 159
Attanagalla, 67, 131
Attaragama Bandara, 135,
Atu Korala, 79, 80
Azavedo, Dom Jeronymo de, 55, 102
Bacon, 128, 156
Badawedili, 5, 50, 78, 80, 81, 153
Baddegama 149
Badulla, 115
Balane Kanda, 44, 117, 119
Balawatara, 136
Baldaeus, Philip, 5
Bana, 103
Bandaranayaka Maha Mudlr, 148, 149, (Don Coenrad Pieter Dias Wijayawardhana, b. 1747, d.)
Barana Ganitaya, 138
Baranama Gabasaka, 139

Barber, 130
Basnayaka, 30, 31. 34, 35, 61
Bastian, Don 85
Bat, 119
Batavia, 1, 4, 12, 23, 52, 55, 56, 60, 61, 63, 69, 71, 73, 76. 85, 93, 103, 106, 113, 121, 147, 149, 164
Batgan, 51
Batticaloa, 17, 22, 43, 98, 120, 121, 124, 142, 150, 152, 153, 162
Bazaar, 82
Becker, Hendrik 48-56, 88
Becket, Tohmas a. 67
Beef, 29, 128
Beer, 128, 156
Beetle, 92
Beligal Korale, 21
Bell, 108
Bengal, 4, 43
Bentara River, 2, 59
Bera, 81
Betel, 52, 155
Bevere de, 53, 54
Bhesajja Manjusa, 65
Bhesajja Nidana, 136
Biyagama, 149
Bibilegama, 21
Bintenne, 96, 104, 118
Blacksmith, 130
Bo, 28, 65, 70
Bogambra, 66
Boscawen, 69
Botany, 24, 25
Brahmin, 138
Brand mark, 3
Breda, 91
Breslau, 89
Bribe, 15, 75, 79, 96, 97
Brick, 131
British 9, 10, 11, 12, 13, 14, 17, 64, 69, 108, 111, 124, 138 144, 147, 150, 152, 160-168
Brohier, 124
Broker, see Elephant.
Buchanan, James, 144, 160, 161
Buddhism, 12, 28, 30, 36, 38, 43, 44, 64, 66, 67, 70, 88, 89, 101, 116, 131, 132, 136, 138, 164
Bulat Surulla, 153
Buffon, 152
Burgher, 6, 25, 130, 154
Burnand, 122, 150
Bystervelt, Henricus Van, 17-19
Cabook, 34,
Calamander, 155
Camel, 56
Campbell, Sir Archibald, 144, 160
Canal, 125, 126, 149, 150, 151
Candle 111
Cane, 125
Cannon, 44, 60, 71, 105, 120, 121
Cape, 101, 113
Capelle, Elias Paravacini de, 91
Cardamom, 84, 85, 120.
Carnatic, 108, 138, 144, 160
Carpenter, 15, 113
Carpet, 110
Carriage, 156
Carron, Francois, 14, 19
Cartwright, 130
Caste, 132
Casti, 75, 118
Cattle, 4, 59
Cavalry, 114
Chain, 18, 113, 129, 148, 156
Chalia, see Cinnamon.
Chank, 14, 71, 83, 152
Changarapillai, Don Philip, 41, 43
Charles, II 9, 15, 19
Chatham, 15
Chayaver, 43
Chetty, 58, 82
Chief, Native, 79, 80, 124
Chilaw, 13, 26, 55, 83, 112, 119, 123, 145, 151, 153
China, 47
Chinna Natchi, 139, 140
Choromandel, 4, 20, 105, 160
Christianity 2, 5, 15, 28, 37, 38, 66, 67, 87-93, 113, 123, 131, 133, 156
Cinnamon, 9, 17, 21-25, 35-39, 44, 51, 55, 59, 63, 66, 67, 77, 85, 86, 97-103, 119, 126, 147, 153, 164
Civil Service, 2, 54, 75, 76, 153
Cloth, see cotton, 129

Clothes 18, 42, 43, 75, 106, 130, 131, 132, 155
Cochin, 147
Cockpit, 131
Coconut, 39, 40, 59, 82, 86, 87, 92, 102, 150, 151, 155.
Coffee, 60, 83, 84, 120, 148, 151
Coinage, 4, 157
Collar, 24, 105
Colombo, 3, 13-19, 22, 26-34, 45, 50, 56, 60, 67, 77, 81, 86, 90-102, 108, 125, 131, 140, 142, 145, 153, 155, 156, 164-169
Comet, 10, 12
Commandeur, 2, 41, 128
Commissioner, 12, 56, 120, 121
Company, 1, 7, 13-16, 45, 49-53, 60-70, 74-84, 97-104, 114, 122, 123, 129, 139, 140, 144, 154.
Conspiracy, 10, 12, 18, 26, 52, 53, 121
Consistory, 92
Constable, 104
Copper, 15, 159
Costa, Don Joan de, 10. (Maamperi Rajapaksa Mudlr.)
Coste, Godfried Leonard de, 119, 121, 125, 129, 130
Cotton, 4, 25, 50, 82, 124, 152, 153, 160
Cornwallis, Lord, 144
Council Political, 2, 19, 60, 61, 73, 90, 92, 107, 161, 164-167
Councillor, Privy, 54
Cowry, 82
Cremation, 31
Crescentie, 40
Crocodile, 33
Crow, 99
Crown, 110, 114
Curtain, 109, 110
Custom, see Justice, Alphandigo
Cyclone, 72
Dagoba, 37, 38
Daimio, 83
Dam, 149
Dane, 9, 19, 147
Dassanayaka, 116, 118
Debt, 3, 151
Decum, 82
Demetagoda, 148
Dewale, 22, 53, 88
Dhammananda, 136
Dharmaka, King. 72
Dharmapala, 38
Dhoney, 51, 124
Digest, see Justice
Director, 45, 112, 113, 159
Dissanayaka, Mudlr, 136
Dissanayaka, Don Simon Wikramaratna 113
Distil, see arrack
Disava, 2, 4, 5, 18, 26, 44, 45, 51, 76, 97, 100, 107, 111, 123, 128, 130, 153
Diver, see Pearl.
Diviture, 149
Dodanwala, 57
Domburg, Diederik Van, 56, 59 60, 93
Don, 133
Doranagama Rala, 67
Dover, 19
Dragoon, 107
Draak, Hendrik, 17
Dravidian, 64, 67, 103
Drink, 6, 29, 87, 95
Drought, 39, 40, 81
Drum, 106, 128
Duflo, Major, 118, 121
Dugganna Rala, 45
Dumbara Rala, 72, 97, 105, 118, 163, 164.
Dunuvila, 136
Dupon, Pierre, 5, 12
Duraroba, 59, 60
Dutch, see Hollander
Dutugemunu, 135
Duty, 25
Dye, 4, 43, 51
Eat, 95
Eck, Baron Van, 108, 112-116, 135
Education, 2, 5, 65, 89, 90, 92-95, 154
Ehelapola, 68, 71, 104
Ekanayaka, Don Constantyn, 104 136, 138

Elephant, 3, 11, 13, 18, 23, 25, 26, 39, 41, 45, 51, 52, 68, 70, 73, 98, 99, 102-106, 114, 115, 121, 124, 129, 135, 152
Embassy, 11, 13, 14, 15, 17, 19, 20, 23, 29, 31, 33, 34, 44, 48, 53, 54, 57, 60, 63, 67, 69, 70, 72, 73, 104, 119, 130, 138, 143
Engineer, 104
England, see British
Erawwawala Adigar, 162
Esala, 70, 71
Eschelskroon, 94, 95
Eswatta, 85
Etbandana, see Elephant
Etiquette, 18, 20
Europe, 10, 45, 49, 52, 75, 83, 88, 93, 94, 104, 120, 121, 144, 155
Eve, 37
Everiyawatta, 148
Evil One, 67
Exchange, 157-159
Factory, 9, 15, 122, 143
Fakir, 28, 82
Falck, Iman Willem, 118, 121-127, 131, 143, 148, 151, 153, 158
Famine, 56, 139, 143
Feber, Colonel, 115, 116, 117
Ferrao, Pedro, 66, 67
Finance, 3, 25, 55, 154
Fines, 5, 59, 94
Fiscal, 58
Fish, 28, 82, 123, 124, 130
Fishery, see Pearl, Ch ank
Flambeau, 107
Flood, 56
Food 155
Footprint, 48
Fornbauer, Major, 162
Freire, Antao Vaz, 77
French, 14, 20, 69, 140, 142, 144, 150, 159, 161
Funeral, 131, 156
Gabadagam, 70, 128
Gabbedature Nayaker, 96
Gajaman Nona, 138
Gajanayaka, see Elephant
Galagedera Pass, 114
Galauda, 11
Galegoda, 103, 104
Galkissa, 153
Galle, 2, 3, 9, 17, 59, 60, 77, 80, 85, 86, 103, 142, 154, 159, 165
Gam Berawaya, 81
Gamble, 131
Gampaha, 70
Gangaboda Pattu, 149
Gangarama, 135
Gannoruwa, 108
Gantalauwa, 150
Gem, 82
George, Fort St, 159
German, 24, 91, 94, 134
Getambe, 44
Ghi, 82
Giants Tank, 3
Gin, 166
Gin Ganga, 149
Giruwaya, 51, 145, 150
Goa, see Christianity
Goens, Rycklof Van, Snr, 6, 7, 12, 13, 15, 21, 124, 148, 151
...... Jnr, 21, 24, 25, 26, 29
Goigama, 62, 130
Goi Vidane, 125
Gollenesse, Julius Valentyn Stein Van, 62, 72, 75, 77, 80, 85, 90, 122
Gopala, 103, 104
Governor, 2, 33, 45, 69, 75, 80, 81, 90, 98, 107, 128, 153
Gowwa, 119
Graaf, Wilhelm Jacob, Vander, 143—160
Grandpass, 149
Greek, 55, 90
Grimm, 25
Gunaratna, 53, (Don Paulo Dias Maha Mudaliyar in 1714)
Haafner, Jacob, 91
Hague, 144
Halberdier, 109
Halle, 24, 91
Hamburg, 73
Hang, 18, 58

Hanguranketta, 11, 17, 20, 23, 27, 28, 31, 56, 62, 115, 121
Hanwella, 30, 80, 85, 105, 120, 146, 163
Hapitigam Korale, 67, 116, 131
Haye, De La, 19, 20
Heere, Gerrit De, 45, 77
Hena, 59, 126
Hendela, 87
Hermann, Paulus, 24
Hewagam Korale, 60, 85
Hikkaduwa, Lake, 149
Hindu, 88, 132
Hippouros, 55
Hobart, Lord, 160,—167
Hollander, 1, 2, 8, 9, 10, 12, 14 16, 24, 29, 83, 89, 90, 93, 95, 100, 111, 112, 141, 154, 158
Horse, 15, 20, 24, 27, 29, 47, 51, 56, 70, 128, 141
Hour glass, 18
Howdah, 116, 119
Hughes, Sir Edward, 140, 142
Hulftsdorp, 2
Hulangomuwa, 56
Humour, 23
Huwandiram, 59, 60
Illangakon, Don Joan Abaya Sriwardhana 113, 121, 136, 137
Image, 66
Impale, 18, 26
Imhoff, Gustaaf Willem Baron Van, 60-67, 74, 76, 77, 80, 85, 90, 93, 94
India, 15, 49, 52, 68, 83, 99, 122, 124
Indigo, 4
Infanta, 9
Infanticide, 8
Inkstand, 18
Irrigation, 123
Isaakz, Claas, 47
Ivory, 120
Jaffna, 1, 2, 3, 24, 40, 41, 43, 45, 47, 51, 52, 56, 66, 68, 76, 77, 82, 90, 91, 98, 117, 124, 125, 131, 139, 141, 152, 156, 163, 164
Jaggery, 82
Japanese, 83
Java, 84
Jesuit, 1, 29
Jewels, 130, 155
Justice, 2, 4, 5, 46, 47, 57, 58, 76, 77, 86, 88, 102, 124, 130, 131
Kabaya, 109
Kadawatu, 8, 54, 57, 98, 128, 145, 147
Kadirana, 148
Kaffir, 27, 150
Kaila Wannia, 7, 22
Kalpitiya, 8, 9, 13, 17, 22, 43, 68, 86, 92, 166
Kalutara, 23, 30, 92, 105, 123, 130, 153
Kanakapulle, 123
Kanda Uda Rata, 8, 26, 65, 108, 124, 136
Kandy, see Senkadagala
Kankesanturai, 40
Kapuwatta, 134
Karachi, 151
Karanduwa, 116, 119, 134
Karatota Dammarama, 138
Karikal, 158
Karti Mangalaya, 28
Karunaratna, 72, 83, 101, 148
Katikawata, 136
Kattakarai, 3, 151
Katugastota, 114
Katukulam Pattu, 113
Katuwana, 1, 137
Kav Mini Kondala, 137
Kav Mini Maldama, 137
Kav Mutu Hara, 137
Kayal Pattanam, 14
Kayman's Gate, 128, 168
Kaymel, 123, 151, 156
Kehelella, 103
Kelani Ganga, 166
Kelaniya, 36, 38, 131, 148
Kendangomuwa, 146
Kevulgama, 134
Kilakarai, 54, 121, 122
Kiramba, 136
Kirimetiyawe Mantri, 65
Kiriwavule Rala, 52
Kirti Sri Raja Sinha, 96-103, 106, 121, 134-141.

Kitchen, 18, 27
Kitul, 103
Knife, 18
Knox, Robert, 9, 26, 29
Kobbyakaduwa, 71
Kollupitiya, 128
Korala, 79, 128
Korale, 79
Korales, Three. 12, 24, 36, 59, 60, 97, 118, 119
Korales, Four, 1, 60, 64, 97, 103, 118, 119.
Korales, Seven, 1, 59, 118, 119, 128, 153.
Koronchi, 156
Korteboom, 167, 168
Kottalbadda, 29
Kotte, 2, 8, 90
Kottiar, 8, 9, 17, 19, 20, 43, 44, 108, 113, 124
Kraal, see Elephant.
Kredit Brieven, 158
Kundasala, 57, 61, 65, 115, 121, 135
Kuttapitiya, 70
Laan, Van der 13
Lacham 40
Lanarolle, Count de, 20, 21, 29, 35
Land, 50, 59, 79, 81, 102
Landraad, see Justice.
Langhansz, Christoph, 89
Language, 77
Lanka, 31, 65, 100
Larin, 40
Lascarin, 5, 25, 44, 58 60, 68, 79, 80, 81, 92, 113, 123, 128, 129, 159
Latin, 72, 90
Law, see Justice.
Leprosy, 87
Lewaya, 30, 39, 119
Lewke Rala, 60, 64, 68, 69, 72
Leyden, 25, 92
Lime, 125
Linnaeus, 25
Lion, 23, 29
Literature, 65, 135-139
Load, 130
London, 9
Loten, Joan Gideon, 72, 73
Louis XIV, 14, 19, 25
Luxemburg, 168
Low Country, see Pata Rata
Madapalli, 41
Madras, 10, 13, 141, 142, 143, 159, 163
Madura, 14, 16, 17, 48, 49, 62, 64, 108
Maduwa, 37
Macartney, Lord, 141
Maecenas, 136
Maetsuycker, 4
Maggelian, Clement, 21, 22
Magul Poruwa, 156
Maha Hatana, 65
Maha Mudaliyar, 72, 81, 97, 113, 149, 155, 159, 160
Maha Nayaka, 35, 37, 103
Maha Oya, 1, 126
Mahara, 128
Maha Sen, 150
Mahastana, see Wimala Dharma
Maha Vihare, 44, 71
Maha Wansa, 100, 101, 117, 135
Maha Weli Ganga, 114
Mahiyangana, 70
Malacca, 118
Malabar, 40, 85, 96, 105, 111, 121
Makaraddaja, 136
Malapala, 78
Malay, 60, 113, 131, 142, 145, 162, 168
Maldives, 83
Maligawa, 44, 57, 134
Malwana, 24, 60
Malwatta, 65, 103, 143
Mampitiya, 64, 68, 86
Manar, 2, 10, 16, 77, 82, 139, 142, 153, 194
Manioc, 151
Maniratna, 137
Maniyagar, 15, 16, 21
Mantota, 3
Mapane, Don Gaspar Nalla, 140

Maradana, 127
Marawila, 151
Marriage, 5, 6, 33, 70, 75, 87, 88, 91, 94, 104, 128, 133, 154, 156
Mascarenhas, Don Philippe, 40
Mask, 39
Matale, 22, 118, 121
Matara, 1, 2, 22, 26, 30, 37, 39, 50, 59, 60, 76, 77, 79, 81-91, 102, 105, 113, 115, 136, 149, 152, 153, 155
Mattamagoda Chetty, 31
Mayoral, 80
Mecklenburg, 132
Medal, 30, 72, 84, 126, 127, 143, 148
Medicine, 25, 61, 65, 87, 136, 150
Megadhuta, 138
Mendis, Anthony, 21
Mendis, Andris, Mudaliyar, 147
Merchant, 2, 100
Merit, 66, 117, 134, 135
Mestico, 33, 75, 87, 91
Meuron, de, 145, 146, 153, 159, 165, 167, 168
Meyden, Van der, 12, 14
Mint, 4
Mitrigala, 85
Mogul, Great, 64
Mohammedan, 91, 103, 123, 128, 131
Mohottala, see Mohottiar
Mohotti Appuhami, see Bandaranayaka.
Mohottiar, 18, 21, 33, 44, 111
Moladanda Rala, 104
Monopoly, see Trade
Moor, 6, 52, 54, 68, 82, 86, 112, 123, 134
Moratota, 136
Moratuwa, 126, 130
Morgen, 126
Moyaart, Anthony, 117
Mudaliyar, 4, 22, 31, 47, 50, 78-81, 104, 127-129, 135, 149, 153, 156
Muhandiram, 44, 80, 128
Mukkuwa, 91, 123
Mulgirigala, 36, 37, 131
Mullativu, 54, 140
Munessaram, 145
Munkottuwe Rala, 136
Musali, 3, 69
Music, 71
Muttetu, 40, 78
Mutwal, 167
Mutturaja Wela, 125,149
Nadukattusami Nayaker, 69
Nagalagama, 143
Nagapatnam, 4, 140, 163
Nagel, Lieut., 139, 140
Nalalpata, 133
Nambukara, 130
Nanayakkara, 89, 130
Narendra, Sinha, Sri Wira, 49, 52-65
Narenappa Nayaker, 64, 68, 69, 96, 104
Natural History, 72
Navadun Korale, 70
Navaratna, (Don Laurens Madere de Basto, Maha Mudlr d. before 1699) 30, 34, 35, 36
(Don Simon Wijayasundera Mudlr) 61
Nawab, see Carnatic
Nayaker, see Madura
Nedimale, 126
Neduntivu, 51
Negombo, 2, 13, 14, 68, 75, 80, 82, 91, 92, 126, 127, 130, 142, 166
Nella Nachchi, 131
Neri, St. Filippe, 66
Net, 124
Netherlands, 49, 54, 140, 161
Nilakobo Sandesaya, 138
Nilambe, 10
Nilapala, 78
Nilwala Ganga, 150
Nimeguen, 25
Nindagama, 70
Notary, 133
Nurenberg, 47
Nuwara Kalawaya, 153
Oliveira, de, 56

Opium, 30
Orange, see William
Orphan, 2, 57
Ordinance, see Justice
Ostenberg, Fort, 140, 162
Overbeek, Govr., 149, 151
Paduwo, 151
Painting, 66
Palanquin, 53, 89
Pali, 65, 134
Palingupana Rala, 104, 134
Pallebeddegama, 138
Pallegampaha, 68, 109
Palansena, 92
Palm leaf, 81
Palmyra, 41, 125
Pamben, 49, 122
Panadura, 140, 149
Panangamam, 7, 139
Panditaratna, 90, (Philip Philipsz Wijayakon, b. 1686)
Paper, 81
Papus, 82
Parakrama Bahu, 70
Parasol, 101
Paraveni, 78
Parawa, 14, 16,
Parchment, 121
Parra, Pedrus Albertus Van der 107
Pas Betal, 167
Pasdun Korale, 80, 85
Patangatyn, 16
Pata Rata, 8, 26 44, 64
Pattiye Bandara, 52, 53
Pearl, 13, 22, 24, 38, 52, 55, 82, 83 138, 139, 144
Pedro, Pt. 10
Pegu, 66
Pehidun, 129
Peliyagoda, 60
Pepper, 75, 85, 120, 123, 148, 151
Perahera, 10, 28, 70
Percivâl, Capt. Robert, 166
Persia, 24, 47, 110
Pettah, 33
Philip, Don, 24
Philip of Spain, 166
Philipsz, Henricus, 90, 121
Physician, see Medicine
Pielat, Jacob Christian, 56-59, 84, 90, 149.
Pilima Talauwa, 104, 145, 162
Pindapatika, 65
Pinhao, Simao, 70
Pin Wattoru, 66
Pipe, 101
Pitfall, 103
Pitigal Korale, 25
Pitti Nayaker, 62
Plague, 72
Plakat, see Justice.
Plantain, 39, 52
Poddalgoda, 53
Poetry, see Literature
Poison, 18, 27,
Polatu Oya, 149
Polaya, 59, 84
Policy, see Company.
Polygar, 64
Polonnaruwa, 70
Pondicherri 159
Poodle, 100
Population, 3, 156
Port, see Trade
Portuguese, 2, 7, 9, 10, 12, 14, 20, 21, 26, 28, 29, 33, 37, 38, 40, 42, 46, 47, 50, 65, 66, 70, 74, 77, 85, 87, 89, 93, 103, 105, 154, 168
Potstili, see Arrack.
Potter, 131
Poya Maluwa, 103
Predicant, 90
Priest, see Buddhism
Printing, 94
Proctor, 76
Protestant, see Christianity
Puliyantivu, 124
Punaryn, 3
Punchi Appuhami, 26, 81, 136
Pusti, 75

Puttalam, 8, 38, 44, 54, 57, 63, 68, 73, 91, 92, 112, 113, 119, 123, 124, 142
Pybus, 108-111, 138, 141
Pyl, Laurens, 25, 29-38, 41, 43
Queen of Raja Sinha, 11, 17, 27
 Wimala Dharma, 47
 Narendra Sinha, 47, 62, 121
 Sri Wijaya, 64, 68, 69
 Kirti Sri, 69, 96, 115, 138
Raad van Justitie, see Justice
Rainer, Commodore, 162
Raja Adhiraja Sinha, 136, 138, 141, 145
Raja Sinha, 7, 9-12, 17-32, 37, 43, 45, 53, 65, 100, 102, 121
 of Sitawaka, 70, 157
Rajakariya, 123
Raket, 143
Rama Nayaka, 96
Rambukwele Unnanse, 134
Rameswaram, 14, 165
Rammalaka Rala, 52, 53, 56
Ramnad, 14, 122
Ran Awuda, 110
Ranchu, 8, 123, 128
Ran Doliya, 27, 141
Rasputin, 67
Rata Sabhawa, 123
Rattan, 129
Raymond, Colonel, 168
Rebellion, 57, 59, 61, 103
Reformed, see Christianity.
Rein, Martin, 114, 117
Relipalan, 110
Renigade, 24, 26
Revenue, 55, 72, 82, 122, 153, 154
Rhee, Thomas van, 38, 45
Rheede, Henrik van, 15, 31, 35, 38.
Rice, 2, 3, 13, 25, 43, 50, 51, 56, 75, 81, 124, 140, 144, 145, 149, 151, 155
Ridi Vihare, 135
Ring, 18
Road, 42, 166
Roman, see Christianity.
Rosewater, 52
Rum, 153
Rumpf, Augustin, 54, 55, 83
Ruwan Ella, 12, 13, 21
Russian, 67
Rymers, 142
Sabaragamuwa, 1, 12, 14, 22, 64, 119, 128, 144
Sack, 128
Safframado, 130
Salpiti Korale, 60, 126
Sali ella, 137
Salsete, 66
Salt, 39, 51, 124, 139, 145
Saltpetre, 118
Samanakkody, 68, 103
Samanala Kanda, 28, 48, 70
Samanera, 65
Samantakuta, see Samanala.
Samarajiwa Lekama, 137
Samarang, 118
Samarasinha, Daniel Alwis, 126, 127
Sangha Raja, 71, 103, 116, 135-138
Sannas, 34, 35, 81
Sanskrit, 65
Saram, Lewis de, see Wijaya Sriwardhana,
 Anthonan de, Wirasinha Sriwardhana, b. circ 1685, d. circ 1752, 81
 Lienderam de, Wijayasinha see Karunaratna
 Johannes de, Wijayasekera, see Abyaratna
Saranankara, see Buddhism, Sangha Raja
Sara Sangrahaya, 65
Saraswati, 137
Scholarchal Commission, see Education.
School, 59, 133
Schreuder, Jan, 73, 74, 76, 79, 81-86, 96-104, 108, 122, 125, 143, 169
Seminary, see Education

Senkadagala, 11, 18, 27, 57, 108, 114, 134
Seven Ports, 14
Seventeen, The, 90
Shark, 83
Shoe, 109
Siam, 69, 71, 72, 103, 135
Silk, 4
Silver, 115, 127
Simons, Cornelis Joan, 46, 47, 49, 87
Sinhale, 8, 9, 10, 19, 82, 84
Sinhalese, 42-50, 60-63, 70, 72, 80, 87, 96-100, 105, 106, 123-130, 145, 154-157
Sitawaka, 1, 17, 24, 70, 117, 146, 157
Sittinamaluwe Dhammajoti, 136
Siyambalape, 148
Siyane Korale, 24, 57, 60, 68, 69, 85, 113, 148
Slave, 3, 43, 83, 89, 98
Slipper, 109
Small Pox, 145, 150
Smuggling, 50, 68, 122, 123
Sowing Master, 51
Spain, 140
Spice, 128
Sparenryk, 107
Sripada, see Samanala.
Sri Rahula, 72
Stadtholder, 161
Stamp, 129
Statute, see Justice.
Stocking, 131
Stuart, Colonel, 162-168
Style, 18
Suffren, Admiral, 141-143
Sugar, 152
Surveyor, 104, 125
Swede, 25
Swiss, 122
Sword, 18, 32, 33, 49, 58, 62, 105, 110, 127
Talavinna, 53
Tamankaduwa, 124
Tamil, see Jaffna
Tampalagamam, 150
Tanayama, 108, 109, 111
Tanjore, 139
Tank, 2, 42, 43
Tavalam, 7, 124
Tavern, 20, 29, 87
Tea, 47
Tennakon, 22—24, 26, 102, 105, 136
Teuton, 2, 4, 6, 32
Thamotharampillai, 122
Thesawalame, see Justice
Thever, 14, 49, 122
Tibbattuwawa, 103, 135
Tilakaratna, 136
Timber, 98, 129
Tippu Sultan, 144
Title, 79
Tobacco, 4, 82, 123, 166
Toddy, 82, 87
Tombo, 51, 77, 79, 93, 102, 105
Tooth Relic, 44, 57, 72, 115, 116, 134
Toppu, 92
Torture, 12, 56, 58
Trade, 8, 9, 11, 15, 16, 44, 48, 55, 56, 57, 63, 67, 68, 86, 112, 120, 122, 151, 157
Travancore, 144
Treaty, 9, 119, 121, 144, 163
Trincomalee, 2, 12, 19, 43, 63, 69, 71, 75, 120, 124, 140, 143, 159, 161, 162
Trumpet, 128
Tumpane, 65
Tuppas, 75, 142
Tutucorin, 14, 16, 61, 144
Tythe, 7, 39, 125
Udagampahe, 68
Udapalata, 18
Udasiya Pattuwa, 53
Udawatukele, 52
Udugoda, 52
Udumale Devi, 62
Udupenkarai, 123
Uliyam, 112, 124, 151
Umbrella, 43

Unambuwe Bandara, 62
Upali Maha Thero, 71
Upasampadawa, 71
Uppu Aru, 125
Utrecht, 90, 119
Vaitilingam Chetty, 152
Vandenberg, Francois, 28
Varnham, Richard, 28
Vaz, Joseph, 66
Veddah, 7, 53
Venloos Bay, 113
Verghonce, 29
Versluys, 56, 85
Vervyk, John, 152
Vidane, 21, 79, 123, 128
Vuyst, Petrus, 55, 56
Wadegai, 62
Walawe Ganga, 1, 2
Wanni, 1, 7, 22, 24, 41, 54, 69, 88, 113, 123, 139, 140, 152, 164
Warana, 131
Wasala, 130
Washerman, 107, 130
Watubadda, 59, 60
Wax, 120
Weaving, 4, 15, 124
Weke, 80
Wehelle, 136
Weligama, 34
Well, 3
Weliwita, 65
Wellala, 4, 41, 42, 131, 133
Weragampita, 138
Weuda, . 114
Wheat, 128
Wheel, 58
Whip, 128
Wig, 56
Wijayapala, 22
Wijaya Raja Sinha, 62—69
Wijaya Sriwardhana, 72, 90
Wijayo, 62
Wijayawardhana, Don Simon, 51, 84, 105
Wikeliya, 26
Wikramasinha Mudlr., 166
William, Fort, 144
William, of Orange, 19
Wimala Dharma Suriya, 10, 12, 33—48
Wine, 29
Winter, Sir Edward, 10, 13
Wisinawaya, 117
Wizard, 22
Wolfs, Johannes Christophel, 132, 133
Wolvendahl, 33, 48, 93
Wurtemberg, 159
Yakada Doliya, 27, 62, 96
Yakdessa, 53
Zoysa, Dines de, 147, 148

BY THE SAME AUTHOR

Ribeiro's Ceilao, 450 pages,	Rs. 5.00
Ceylon, the Portuguese Era, 2 vols., with Maps and Illustrations, 1250 pages,	Rs. 15.00

NEARLY READY

Ceylon and the Portuguese, 1505—1658.